To Alexx
My very good frien[d]
with my very best leg[ards]
Captain Eric Kemp M.M.F.G.

A MASTER MARINER
OF THE 20TH CENTURY

Captain John Kemp MBE –

A
MASTER MARINER
OF THE
20TH CENTURY

Eric Kemp

UNITED WRITERS
Cornwall

UNITED WRITERS PUBLICATIONS LTD
Ailsa, Castle Gate, Penzance, Cornwall.

British Library Cataloguing in Publication Data:
A catalogue record for this book is
available from the British Library.

ISBN 1 85200 102 X

Printed in Great Britain by
United Writers Publications Ltd
Cornwall.

Acknowledgements

I would like to place on record my thanks to my long-suffering wife who has had to put up with me during the writing of this book, Jeremy my son, who helped with the photographs, and all those who have encouraged and prodded me into making the effort necessary to record the interesting life of my father.

My thanks also go to Ian Bell, Tom Richards, Margaret and Brian Stevens, Douglas Williams, Roy East and the St. Ives Museum, all of whom have been helpful along the way.

Acknowledgement and thanks are also given to the following for use of photographs within this book:

National Museums & Galleries of Northern Ireland, Ulster Folk and Transport Museum.

The Comley Collection.

Leslie Potton of St. Ives.

The St. Ives *Times and Echo*.

Sam Bennetts.

Preface

How well does a man know his father? In his younger days, the son knows the outline of his father's character and mode of life. But how much does he know?

My father, a world-travelled master mariner, was often away from his home in St. Ives, the Cornish fishing port just a few miles from Land's End, for years at a time. So there were many details about his life-style and experiences of which I had only an outline knowledge.

My most vivid memory was of him standing in the door of a departing railway carriage waving his handkerchief. As the train pulled away from the station, the handkerchief would be withdrawn and then reappear on the other side of the train before it disappeared out of my sight.

In was only in his later years that I got to know him well and to learn of his fascinating experiences. His life covered our twentieth century and is now part of our maritime history.

His journey of life, and also that of my mother, is now over, but he left me a vast wealth of detail in the extensive records, notes, and diaries, which through the years he had carefully preserved.

Together with my memories and other details gleaned from the family, it all makes a fascinating tale about the life of a man who truly loved the sea. It is a story which I hope you, the reader, may well find totally absorbing.

It took men of John Kemp's ability, together with the

dedication of wives like Ann, to create the best Merchant and Royal Navies the world has ever seen. I miss them both very much indeed, for as the captain of the *Ashanti Palm* said on meeting him, "They don't make them like that anymore."

Contents

1
In the Beginning

November in the year 1905 was just a routine month for the people of St. Ives. A schooner, *Welcome Home*, was stranded on the treacherous Hayle Bar, a shifting sand bank to the south end of the bay that had been all too often the stormy graveyard of other ships down the years.

Those on board had been taken off by lifeboat, for the crew of which it was just another rescue. Later the vessel was to be refloated to resume trading.

Detailed in the local paper were the latest worldwide positions of the twenty-five ships of the Hain Steamship Company based in the town, and the twelve ships of the Chellew Company based in Truro. These were of intense interest to the townspeople, as they all knew many of the crews on the ships personally.

In the town itself the gossip centred on a poor herring season and the second most important factor in the economy of St. Ives, the price then being obtained by the locally mined tin. Also, would there be money for the harbour improvement scheme which had been argued about over and over again in the local council chamber?

For much of this gossip there was a focal meeting place, almost a town parliament: Sam Kemp's barber's shop on the harbour front. On Saturdays in particular, the discussion would go on and on as the local fishermen sat waiting for a shave, given at a penny a time, so they would look spruce for Sunday worship. Their salt cake stubbles, after days at sea, would never have been right for church or chapel.

On Saturday the twelfth of November, however, Sam's mind dwelt on a more demanding event, the birth of his second son, destined eventually to be a boy of spirit and courage.

"What are ee going to call en Sam?" the men kept asking as they congratulated the hairdresser on the new arrival.

"John. We're naming him John," Sam replied, and John it was to be.

Sam's shop was located behind Doble's Wall, a low wall with gaps in it, which made it necessary for wooden boards to be put in place when tides were high. This was essential for the safety of Sam's family, which was eventually to include five daughters as well as two sons, with part of their living accommodation above the shop but the rest at the back on ground level. In the tough conditions of those days, although crowded, it was a reasonable place to live.

For a boy who grew to be enchanted by the sea there was always something going on to capture his interest, with top sailed schooners discharging coal, cement or timber into horse drawn carts and the arrival and departure of the herring or mackerel fleets under sail.

Before the First World War, there could be six hundred or more vessels of all shapes and sizes in the harbour area, and the town's narrow streets would be cluttered with carts carrying fish catches to the railway station.

Extra horses were kept at two points along the route of these carts to help toiling animals get up the hills. At these locations John would wait in his free time to get the privilege of leading the horses back to the bottom of the hill. This was the start of a love affair with the sturdy animals, which served him well in later life.

When John was four the family moved to Molteno Place in the part of the town known as upalong, close to the Trenwith tin mine. Close by lived a wealthy spinster named Miss Treweeke Stevens, often to be seen in her pony and jingle, a small locally built riding cart similar to a surrey.

To Miss Treweeke many of the local boys were merely urchins, much to be avoided. But in John she saw something special and, a few years later, he was allowed to take the reins of her pony and drive her around the countryside. He would go home rewarded with a piece of cake and still clean and tidy.

On other days he would slide down the steep mine dumps of red arsenic spoil above his home, ripping the seat out of his trousers, or hang on to the odd fish lorry tailgate, grazing his legs and arms as he fell off. All to the despair of his mother who needed to watch the pennies in such hard times and was never slow to administer the odd heavy smack.

She was also quick to aim a missile, such as a pebble, when her errant brood annoyed her. On one occasion her misjudged throw shattered the greenhouse in the garden: "Look what you have made me do," she yelled. "I shall tell your father it was all your fault!"

Sam, after a hard day's work in his barber's shop, used his belt to enforce family discipline and banished John, by then with his backside smarting, to his room. Mary, her conscience troubling her, for she was the real culprit, decided half an hour later to see if John was all right. The bedroom window was open and her young son had disappeared down the drainpipe to play with his mates on nearby Porthminster beach, without a care in the world. His father soon found him and he was marched back home for another dose of the leather belt.

In school, John and trouble were frequent pals. Fights with other boys and pulling the hair of a little girl, Ann Uren, who sat in the desk in front of him, all brought more beatings from the severe headmaster. Often his father backed up the punishment at school with more of the same.

This harsh treatment, plus bullying from his eldest brother, also called Sam and some seven years his senior, had the effect of producing a hardened self-reliant young man with a burning ambition to make his own way in life.

He was, however, somewhat penalised by the problems of schooling during the First World War. His class at that time had seventy pupils because all the younger teachers had been called away to fight. So John's education, by the time he left school at fourteen, was little more than a basic understanding of the three Rs, and an ability to defend himself in any situation of violence. Hardly the right training for a boy who would wish to be a Master Mariner in years to come.

He did, though, have one shattering lesson about the constant threat of danger in a life at sea:

William Carbines, a likeable nineteen-year-old St. Ives lad, collected a parcel from the Kemp home to deliver to relatives in America. The parcel was not delivered – William Carbines never arrived in the United States. He perished as the ill-fated liner *Titanic* went down in the Atlantic after striking an iceberg. His body was returned to St. Ives, where the Kemp family joined hundreds of other sorrowing townsfolk at the funeral. Many years later John could remember the solemn occasion and the remarks about so many dying at sea on the ill-fated liner.

There was also the experience of helping with the launch and recovery of the local lifeboat whenever it was called out to a vessel in trouble. As the rockets were fired ordering the crew to the lifeboat house, the youngsters in the town gathered there as well. At that time the boat, on its heavy carriage called 'James Stevens No 10', had to be hauled by horses down to the beach and across the sand to get afloat.

John's love of horses and his skill in handling them made him a natural to lead them into the sea as men and animals struggled to get the boat afloat. He soon learned what ropes sodden with seawater and rain could do to tender young hands. It was all a very testing way in which to prepare for a life of hard work which was soon to follow.

John got his first job before he left school, looking after a pony and trap owned by a farmer who had a habit of taking more than enough of the local brewed ale in the bar of one of the town's leading hotels. While the farmer drank on, it was John's job to ensure that no one damaged the trap and the pony didn't bolt.

At closing time the farmer would stagger from the bar and invariably fail in his effort to climb into the trap, and the second part of John's job was to heave him into the driver's seat.

Without that help, most nights the farmer would not have made it, and he was just as reliant on the intelligence of the pony, which was by then cold from standing about for hour after hour and braying away to show how keen it was to get back to its stable. One smart smack on his backside from John and the pony, knowing well his way home, would set off at a determined trot.

John was already showing wisdom beyond his years, as he had negotiated a payment of sixpence in advance and did not have to worry about payment as the trap disappeared into the night. He would normally have already enjoyed a good portion of fish and chips from the proceeds.

School-days eventually came to an end, but there was no enthusiastic leaving endorsement for John from his headmaster. Instead there was a stern prediction: "Kemp, you'll never do any good in your life, you're too much of a rebel."

2

A Butcher's Boy

John's father Sam scratched his head with some concern as with his wife Mary he discussed their younger son's future.

"It's no good thinking he can come into the shop," Sam said. "I can never keep him there. He dislikes putting lather on the beards and as soon as I am distracted he's gone. I have taught him to cut hair but he'll never be really good at it."

Mary replied, "How about his way with animals? Something to do with animals or a farm perhaps?"

"Well, Tom Trevorrow needs a butcher's boy for slaughter work. That could suit him."

That was Sam's quick reply. And it was the week after leaving school that John started at Mr Trevorrow's shop as a butcher's boy at the tender age of fourteen.

"Now, my boy," Trevorrow said, "you'll have to work hard to justify your wages. I'll take you to farms and markets like Helston, where I buy the heifers, and then you will walk them back to St. Ives and help me kill them. Do you think you can do that?"

John replied, "Yes sir. Are we going today?"

"Now wait a minute," said the butcher, startled at John's eagerness, "you will have to learn the cuts of beef and help to sell it in the shop, and your wage will be fifteen shillings a week to start."

"That's all right by me," said John.

So John would be taken in a pony and trap to Helston, some fifteen miles away, and soon after would drive a heifer from the market along the narrow lanes bordered by high Cornish hedges. Sometimes farmers or walkers would leave the gates to fields open and the heifer would stray off the lane, then a chase would occur, with John sometimes having to wade through mud and streams to round the animal up. Finally, he would arrive back in St. Ives where he'd take part in the killing of the animal, with the fresh blood running over his boots as the slaughter took place. After cutting it up he would deliver the carcass to the shop in the main street, before assisting in the butchering, selling and delivery of the meat to the customers.

At first all went well and John worked really hard achieving a good relationship with Trevorrow. A couple of months after starting the job Trevorrow met him as he arrived at the slaughter-house with a heifer from an outlying farm. The rain was torrenting down and John was soaked to the skin but still very cheerful.

"Now John," Trevorrow said, "I'm really pleased with your work and am going to pay you a further half crown a week."

Trevorrow was astounded at his butcher boy's response. John didn't seem too keen.

"That wouldn't do me much good, Mr Trevorrow," he said. "My mother takes all but two shillings now. If she heard about it she would take the whole two shillings and even the sixpence. I would not get any extra at all."

"In that case, my boy," said the butcher, "we won't tell her, will we?"

Unfortunately trouble was brewing and the happy progress of young Kemp was soon to be halted. Even though after the war trade was good and profits improving, the problem with Tom Trevorrow was that he was not very good at paper work and relied on his sister to keep the accounts.

One day, while John was in the shop, the sister entered as the butcher was paying a supplier out of the till. As soon as the shop was quiet she turned on Tom and gave him a lecture on accounts.

She told him in no uncertain fashion: "All money in the till is to be banked. I'm fed up trying to balance the books while you do this sort of thing."

John was standing in the back of the shop as the harassed butcher lost his temper with the hectoring woman in front of him and shouted at her at the top of his voice, "I've had enough of this!" He then hurled a tasty set of chops at his sister. His aim was not good; the chops sailed through the doorway into the street. She retaliated with some sausages, and an infamous row got under way right in front of John.

All too soon a curious crowd gathered outside the shop and cats and dogs mingled to partake of the chops and sausages. It was not often that the pets of St. Ives had such a glorious feast.

John was deputed to clean up the mess and also had to take the angry words of his boss as he tried to calm down after his sister had left.

Then another event occurred, which was to change everything. Tom hired his nephew, his sister's son, as a butcher's boy and that really spelled trouble for John. As a member of the family the nephew thought he could order his fellow butcher's boy around. After a number of upsets the two boys squared up to one another. The chosen scene for this was the abattoir one evening. All the meat had been removed but the blood of the animals slaughtered a couple of hours before still remained. Both boys were fighting furiously when they fell into the mess just as Mr Trevorrow came in.

Furious at the sight he pulled them apart. He sent his nephew home with a clout on the ear.

Then he turned to John with a pained look on his face, but in a gentle voice said, "Now look here, my boy, you have worked really well for me but he's family. His mother didn't like you being in the shop while we were arguing and now, after this event, she will be even worse. I am sorry but I've got to live with my family, so you had better find a job elsewhere."

John made his way home with his last pay packet, to face the coming furious wrath of his father and mother.

"You're always in trouble fighting," his mother said, "will you never learn?"

Ignoring John's protests that it was not his fault, she sat down with her husband once more to discuss the worrying problem of her youngest son's future employment.

Sam, John's elder brother, had gone to sea six years before as an apprentice with the St. Ives shipping company Hain's before joining the China customs service. Mary wanted John to join the same company in the same way. She argued: "It'll force him to grow up and will get him off our hands."

Sam was not so sure. "That's all very well Mary, but it's an expensive operation to send the boy away to sea as an apprentice," he complained. "The other one needed an ordinary uniform and also a tropical one, there were oilskins, seaboots, plates, mug, knives and forks and footwear, not to mention working gear. Then we will have to provide a ten pound bond to the company for his good behaviour, I'm not sure we can afford it."

But Mary had had enough. She was the one who really ruled the family: This young man was going to sea and her long-suffering husband just had no option but to accept what she said and find the money.

John was summoned into the front room to face his father.

"Now, my boy, your mother and I have had a talk and you're going to sea as an apprentice in Hain's."

John only half listened as his mother, in a tone of finality, announced, "You have always liked the sea and now is your chance to see the world."

Next morning, dressed in his best suit, face scrubbed and looking like a young angel, he was taken by his mother to the office of the Hain Steamship Company in what is now called Tregenna Place but was then called the Green Court.

The Hain Steamship Company had started from humble beginnings in 1816. The first Edward Hain had a third share in a fishing lugger *Dasher*. By 1879 the company had purchased its first steamship the SS *Trewidden*. In 1917, following the death of the then chairman Sir Edward Hain, grandson of the founder, the company owned twenty-three ships and was sold to the P & O Steam Navigation Company.

Although now owned by a London Company, Hain's staffing was still managed from its St. Ives office, and in 1920 its fleet had risen to some forty-three ships. Most of the vessels carried six apprentices and there was a continuing need to recruit. They worked very hard and long hours but still the parents had to provide some of the wages during their four-year contract. They were a source of cheap labour and, as officers in training, could be relied on to take responsibility when needed.

So, as his mother ushered him towards the desk of the company secretary, a Mr William Cogar, she was really pushing at an open door. Cogar knew the Kemp family very well, John's father was his barber. Cogar's opening words were cautious in response to Mary Kemp's explanation of their reason for seeing him.

Looking over his desk he said in a doubtful voice, "Your son is rather small for someone going to sea, Mary."

"He'll grow," she replied with firm conviction.

"Well I don't know," said Cogar. "He left school at fourteen and hasn't had much education."

Not in the least daunted Mary asserted, "He'll learn, just as other apprentices do when they go to sea."

"Well let's see now," said Mr Cogar. "You must take an eye test and then I will let you know."

As it turned out the test was not a conventional one, it consisted of identifying a number of coloured pieces of string. Then next day John, together with his father and mother, were summoned to the company office to hear the good news and be present at the signing of indentures for the newest apprentice in the Hain Company.

The bond of ten pounds was paid in cash and the company promised to pay its latest apprentice five pounds in the first year, seven pounds ten shillings in the second year, twelve pounds ten shillings and twenty pounds in subsequent years. Provided he gave total satisfaction throughout this period he would receive a bonus of five pounds at the end of his apprenticeship.

John promised to faithfully serve the captain of any ship he was serving in and there was legalised jargon about his responsibilities to others in the company, and that he must obey all their lawful orders: He would keep their secrets, and give them true accounts of money entrusted to his care. He would not waste, damage or embezzle their goods, or absent himself without leave from their service. He was not to play unlawful games nor frequent taverns or ale-houses.

He had to provide for himself wearing apparel, sea bedding and necessaries. To this end the company provided a list of gear that the new apprentice would need. Should the company provide any of these it could deduct the cost from his wages. As well as wages the company undertook to provide meat, drink, lodging, washing, medicine and medical assistance. It also provided a cap and badge plus uniform buttons, which were pressed into use almost at once.

Strange as it now may seem, at the age of fifteen John Kemp had never worn long trousers. Now at Simpson's tailor's shop in St. Ives he was provided with his Merchant Navy uniform. The tailor, a Mr Rowe, was instructed by Mary, "Make the uniform with plenty of room for a growing lad mind." The suit cost his already hard up father four pounds seventeen shillings and sixpence.

Just before Christmas 1920 John received a letter telling him to join the steamship *Trevessa* at the John Redhead shipyard in South Shields on the River Tyne. Two weeks later he set off from St. Ives railway station to join his first ship. His baggage consisted of a large sea-bag and portmanteau with as much gear as his parents could afford; bedding, towels, clothes, matches, soap and so on. Mary was at the station to see him off with the words: "Work hard and don't come back to me if you get into trouble."

Then John watched the small station disappear out of sight for the first of very many times in his life.

After a short journey on the branch line he joined the main line train at St. Erth. Here he met the first of his companions for the next two years – Eric Goddard from St. Martins in the Isles of Scilly, also a first trip apprentice. At Hayle, where he lived, Mr John Daniel, the third officer of the *Trevessa*, joined them both.

21

He had just passed his second mate's ticket after completing his indentured time with Hain's. As the experienced one of the party he was able to shepherd the two boys on their long journey to South Shields. Changing trains at Bristol, Crewe and Newcastle they arrived twenty-eight hours later.

Here the experience of the third officer came in useful. He advised, "I should eat now boys, the grub on the ship is plain so it's best to get some shore food while we can." So they stopped for a cooked breakfast outside the station before getting a taxi to the shipyard. It was to be a breakfast John would remember with relish in the coming months.

3

At Sea at Last

SS *Trevessa* was built in Flensburg, Germany, as the *Imkenturm*, for the German Liner Company Hansa Line in 1909. The ship had been interned in the First World War at Surabaya in Java for four years and her general condition had deteriorated as a result. In 1919 the vessel was handed over to the British Government as a war prize. Initially managed by the British India Company, she was purchased for the Hain Line from the Government in 1920 for £86,000. The coming voyage was her first for the owners and therefore all the crew were new on board. A 5,004 gross ton freighter, she was 401 feet long with a beam of 52 feet 7 inches and a loaded draft of 28 feet 3 inches. Her four cylinder steam reciprocating engine gave her a speed of 11 knots. *Trevessa* had four main holds as well as a small tonnage hatch. She carried 7,000 tons of cargo and 700 tons of bunker coal, which was often augmented by carrying coal in any cargo space that was empty or even on the open deck if that was not available.

Now berthed in a dry dock covered with all the oil, rubbish and dirt of a refit, without power or heat, she was hardly a welcoming sight to those joining her for the first time.

At first all John could see was the masts and a black funnel with a massive H painted in white. Then the accommodation and bridge appeared just above the dry dock level. It came as a shock to realise that being in the dry dock the ship was below the level on which he was standing.

However, to the young John she looked a wonderful sight as he struggled down the gangway with his gear on to the cluttered deck. Here he met a fellow apprentice, Douglas Bell, who gave them a cheerful welcome:

"Good cabins aboard here but the cook is not up to much," was his opening sentence.

He helped John and Eric to their small double berth cabin amidships – their home for the next two years. Two to a cabin was unusual, normally all six slept together. But the boys had no mess room and ate from boards balanced on their knees. Not for them the luxury of a saloon with tables and chairs and crockery. Not even a wash-basin; ablutions were carried out on deck. While in harbour the only light at night was an oil lantern. Yet John Kemp was impressed, for here was a route to a better life than his parents had ever known. As he was introduced to Captain Gibson he could, in his own mind's eye, see himself dressed in a captain's uniform one day.

Captain Gibson commanded a crew of forty-four on the *Trevessa* and was an impressive man in his own right with a full ginger beard and jutting chin. Although not tall, standing with his legs apart and his hands clasped behind his back he would dominate anyone who stood in front of him. Normally he lived a solitary life on the ship, only eating with the officers on Sunday. Otherwise, apart from his duties, he kept himself to himself. He was a native of Coverack, near Falmouth, and had served all his time in the Hain Steamship Company. During the First World War he had been a prisoner on the German raider *Emden* after his vessel had been torpedoed. Following his release in 1918 he had been appointed master of the *Tresillian,* an old ship built in 1899 and a complete contrast to the modern ship he now commanded.

Now he gave the new apprentices a pep talk.

"I expect my orders and those of my officers to be carried out without question," he boomed. "You are expected to learn the seafaring trade on my ship and so I advise you to study hard. If you get out of line you will be put on bread and water until I'm satisfied you've learned your lesson."

The Kemp family home and barber's shop in St. Ives, 1905.

Home Fleet in St. Ives Bay, c.1921.

St. Ives fishing fleet in John Kemp's boyhood.

The ill-fated SS *Trevessa*.

Survivors of the *Trevessa* on their way home from Mauritius in the Indian Ocean, 1923.

A burial at sea in the Atlantic from the SS *Trebartha*.

Loading zinc ore on the SS *Trebartha* at Port Pirie
in Australia, 1924.

SS *Trevean* soccer team in 1927.
John Kemp front row left.

Third mate John Kemp on the SS *Bangalore*,
passing Cape Vincent in 1929.

John Kemp achieves his Master's Certificate, 21st Nov. 1930.

Honeymoon couple John and Ann in Falmouth, 1931.

SS *Burdwan* dropping the pilot on leaving Malta, 1933.

Ship's cargo to Bombay on SS *Burdwan*
care of Second Mate John Kemp, 1933.

SS *Burdwan* passing HMS *Diamond* at Aden in 1934.

SS *Burdwan* during heavy weather in the Bay of Biscay, 1935.

This proved a very effective way of controlling John Kemp who always did like his food. Indeed from then on he was rarely in trouble.

Following this lecture the boys were sent down to the first mate Mr Williams, who actually came from St. Ives and whose sister Mrs Leddra owned a local chemist shop which still exists in Fore Street today. Mr Williams was in control of the apprentices and he instructed them as to their daily tasks.

"Now, my lads, just clean your cabin today, you start tomorrow morning at seven. The senior apprentice will let you know your jobs then."

First thing next morning it was a case of cleaning the bridge and chart room before breakfast, then on to load stores and clean the spaces where repairs had been completed.

Some five days after John joining, preparations began for the *Trevessa* to leave the dry dock. Down below in the stoke hold the fires were lit in the boilers to raise steam.

During those five days John was getting to know his new companions and masters. Of particular interest were the Cornishmen: Serving as second mate was Mr Rouncefield who lived in Draycott Terrace, St. Ives and, of course, Mr Daniel the third mate who had travelled up with him from Hayle. These two had many of their own duties but at times they did have an apprentice to help them. They also passed on helpful information on the skills needed to rise in their chosen profession, although it was already clear to John that he would have to acquire books and other practical information to get that captain's uniform one day. His wages were not going to be enough to achieve this aim and that was a problem which exercised his brain in these early days.

Normally in charge of the boys for the rough work like cleaning the cargo holds was the bosun Paul Quick, who also came from St. Ives and was a worshipper at the Primitive Chapel there. He was a strict disciplinarian in every sense of the word and expected the boys to work even harder than his seamen.

Two of the able seamen, Mr Peters and Mr Craze, were also from John's hometown. They, like many fishermen, signed to go to sea when times were bad locally.

c

Lastly, also from St. Ives, was the mess room steward Mr Earnest Humphries, who looked after the officers and had little to do with the apprentices.

Of the six apprentices only Eric Goddard and John came from Cornwall. Douglas Bell and David Donaldson came from Glasgow, while Walter Courtney came from Riegate in Surrey and John Tanner came from Gravesend in Kent.

Trevessa had four engineers: two from South Shields and one from Wales and Scotland respectively. The rest of the crew were chosen by the chief officer at the shipping office and were mainly Tynesiders.

By the sixth morning the steam crept into the deck lines with a loud banging noise and the ship was really coming to life. Early in the morning the water from the river had been allowed to run into the dock. Now, without cargo in her holds and very little coal in her bunkers, she floated well above the surrounding buildings. A strong breeze blew in from the North Sea and two tugs waited at the dock entrance. Up above the bridge flew the pilot flag and the crew stood by to move the ship to a nearby berth to load bunkers and prepare for sea.

John was on the stern helping with the mooring ropes and taking the tug's towrope when he experienced the thrill of the ship moving for the first time. He listened to the shouted orders from the pilot and the blasts on the ship's siren as she shifted on to the riverside berth.

Now the excitement mounted as the really hard job of stowing 900 tons of good steam bunker coal to feed the ship's boiler fires began. At South Shields the coal was tipped from a chute into the ship. Apprentices, stripped to the waist and covered in the grimy dust, choked and coughed as they shovelled and trimmed the coal into the amidships bunker hatches and in the number three hold.

The conditions were testing these young people. The weather was very cold, with ice on the deck on which you had to wash and clean up afterwards.

Cleanliness was very important to all mariners at that time and any apprentice who did not keep himself clean was in real trouble. One remedy used on the ship in those days, was to strip the offender and scrub him with deck brooms and seawater. This did not happen to John, but one of his companions suffered this punishment during the voyage.

Following this the ship was prepared for a general cargo and the crew and apprentices worked the last few hours alongside, laying rough timber to cover the ship's steel plates and protect the cargo they were shortly to load on the Continent.

Then, after some engine trials and correction of the ship's compass, the *Trevessa* disembarked a dockyard party of various workmen including the compass adjuster and the pilot, at the entrance to the River Tyne. John helped getting the pilot ladder hung over the ship's side and in lowering the gear onto the deck of the pilot-boat. Now, with three long blasts on her siren, she left the river and turned into the freshening southerly wind to head for Hamburg. John waved to the disappearing boat and turned to stowing the ladder and starting a whole new life with all the enthusiasm of youth.

The three-day voyage proved a difficult one, with strong gale force winds giving the *Trevessa* a poor passage to the entrance of the River Elbe. As the vessel pitched and rolled her way across the North Sea the work on cleaning her still continued. Five of the six apprentices were seasick, John being the exception.

"Part of the job," was the reply of the chief officer when the senior apprentice complained. "You get with it or you will be up to see the Master, my son."

So, in the company of the three other first trippers, John spent his time cleaning the ship's brass work on the stern poop deck during daylight hours.

Working four hours on and four hours off, night watches were spent keeping a lookout making tea and steering the ship. To change the hours around two special dog-watches were kept. These consisted of two hours each, between four and eight in the afternoon, to rotate the times every two days.

The brass on the poop deck was mainly on the emergency wheel and compass, and had been untouched for more than four years. It proved a foul job, as the vessel rolled and pitched in the seaway and the propeller thrashed as it came out of the water causing the steamer to vibrate violently. Then as the wind swung to the North the temperature began to fall alarmingly, a good test indeed to see if these boys were the material to make future officers of the Merchant Navy.

The *Trevessa* had been chartered by the British India Company to load on the Continent for India. Her cargo consisted of crates of machinery, steel-work, salt, sugar and foodstuffs such as cheeses, biscuits, beer, furniture and even bullion. Her loading ports as well as Hamburg were Antwerp, Rotterdam and Marseille.

During this time the boys became used to all sorts of hours of work. These left them exhausted and not having the time to see any of the sights of the ports they visited. After long hours at stations moving the vessel into and out of continental ports, they then worked the same hours as the dockers, loading the cargo. They kept watch in the holds and personally checked all vulnerable cargo such as bullion, beer and cigarettes into secure lockers built in the 'tween-decks of the vessel.

They tended and fixed the movable lights and locked the hatches with iron bars and padlocks at the end of each working day. The officers supervised these jobs and they worked alongside the apprentices on the valuable cargo checks and security duties.

In the meantime John had found at least a partial answer to his money problems. Using the experience gained in his father's shop he gave the crew haircuts for a small fee.

His first customer was the bosun Paul Quick. Coming from St. Ives and knowing John's father, he asked John, "Will ee cut my hair boy?" as they passed Gibraltar. On completion of the task he remarked, "That's a good job for a young boy. Here is tuppence."

By the time the ship had left Marseille, those boys who joined in South Shields had become men. Their main consideration at this time was food. Every three weeks they were issued with some basic stores, including a tin of condensed milk, a ration of sugar, tea, jam, a bar of soap and a very large jar of pickles for all to share. Care was needed with the milk and sugar, as they quickly became the targets of the cockroaches, which infested the

28

accommodation. John used to puncture his tin twice with holes on either side of the top, then after using his ration for the day he would plug the holes with small wooden plugs. The tin was then placed in a larger tin together with the sugar and wrapped tightly with cloth and stowed in his sea bag. This method proved effective and ensured he had some left towards the end of the ration period, which is more than can be said for some of the other apprentices. Indeed on some occasions fights broke out because some had milk and some had not.

In the case of the pickles, all shared from the same jar and this did lead to trouble on one occasion. While working on deck under the supervision of the bosun one of the lads asked to be excused to go to the toilet. He was away for a long time and eventually the bosun said to John, "Go and find out what that boy is doing."

The lad was sitting in his cabin eating the pickles, and this led to him having to visit the captain's cabin:

"You are on bread and water for three days," stormed Captain Gibson. Then, to Mr Williams, "It is quite clear to me that the apprentices have too many pickles, half the ration for all of them at once mister."

While the vessel was on short trips between ports fresh vegetables were available, but as the time at sea lengthened into longer hauls these soon disappeared. Salt beef and pork were stowed on the ship in oak barrels, with beef served during the week and the delicacy of pork on Sundays. Another dish served up at tea times was a hash consisting of corned beef mixed with biscuits, old potatoes and any other leftovers, and fried. Breakfast consisted mainly of unsweetened porridge with salt, while one egg and a ration of bacon was served once a week. Friday would see dried Newfoundland cod on the menu as an alternative to beef; this was so salty that much of it went back over the ship's side.

In port, on rare occasions, if the conduct of the apprentices was to the captain's liking, they were allowed to have chicken. If not, the salt beef was served in its place.

Baking bread was difficult with the ship rolling or pitching in the seaway. Much depended on the cook and his skill with baking and making do with what was available. At this time the cook's poor cooking became the subject of much argument between crew-members. During these times the crew lived on a kind of baked biscuit and this led to members of the crew approaching Captain Gibson to complain.

"I take your views very seriously. I will inspect the food at once," he would say drawing himself up to his full height.

He would then proceed to the galley, followed by the complaining seamen. Then he usually sampled some of the food in front of the crew and would dismiss the complaint with the words, "Tastes excellent to me. If I can eat it so can you." Which of course did not please the disgruntled crew.

Apprentices did not take part in these rituals – they suffered too much bread and water as it was!

4

East of Suez
for the First Time

Now well into February 1921, the *Trevessa* approached Port Said at the entrance to the Suez Canal and waited there for a convoy south to the Red Sea. Already the climate was hot and the cold weather gear had been put away, as the crew enjoyed the sights of this Egyptian port.

However, work was the first order of the day, and being an ex-German ship the *Trevessa* carried her own Suez Canal searchlight. So on arrival the crew had to manhandle the heavy light from its storeroom in the forepeak up to the fo'c'sle. Here it was hung over the bow and would be used to pick up the navigation marks at night as the vessel proceeded through the canal. Before the canal passage two local electricians came on board to tend this light. Also four boatmen brought two small rowing boats which were used to take mooring lines ashore to the side of the canal if the convoy should stop.

While waiting for a convoy and moored at the northern end of the canal, local boats came to trade and barter with exotic leather goods and other items suitable for the folks back home. Here John watched the more experienced officers bargaining and getting big price reductions for their trouble.

Soon an English pilot came aboard from the Suez Canal Company (British & French owned) who controlled all

31

movement in the canal, and *Trevessa* commenced her passage southwards through the canal.

Despite the intense heat of over a hundred degrees, Captain Gibson insisted that the apprentices go to stations in the canal in their long white uniforms.

"My ship is a smart one," he would insist, "apprentices are officers and should dress at stations as if they were."

There is no doubt that the boys suffered a great deal from the heat while going through the canal; indeed there was only marginal relief at night after the sun had gone down.

On the trip south the vessels paused in the Bitter Lakes to change pilots at Ismailia, then some twenty-four hours later sailed through the port of Suez. Here the pilot, boatmen and boats were disembarked and the canal light was put back into its storeroom until next time.

Then out into the Gulf of Suez where the boys could see the majestic shoreline with all the colours of yellow, purple, red and brown slipping by. However, that was scant comfort as the temperature soared to over a hundred and ten degrees and the whole ship seemed to radiate heat wherever you went. At the entrance to the Gulf of Suez the ship passed by The Brothers lighthouse and the coastline then disappeared into the haze. With a following wind and extreme heat the boys slept on deck to catch what cool air there was during the hours of darkness.

Two days later saw the ship in Port Sudan discharging the first items of cargo. Below decks during the day the heat was tremendous and the boys had to work on security watch in relays. But as the cargo was confined to only two of the hatches this allowed the work to be shared. During this time Douglas Bell and John noticed the large number of fish swimming close to the ship.

"I'm going to make up a fishing line," said Douglas.

"Yes," said John, "and we can use some of that salt cod as bait."

They made up two fishing lines and caught a number of fine fish. These made a very welcome change to the diet and helped mitigate the extreme conditions in the port. Despite comments of 'mad dogs in the midday sun' from their mates it was not long

32

before they were doing the same thing.

Trevessa was soon on her way again and approaching the southern end of the Red Sea. There she paused at the small bunkering station on the island of Perim in the Indian Ocean. Here, under British protection, a supply of bunkering coal existed especially for steamships. From time to time a ship would be chartered to run a full cargo of coal to the island for this purpose. A British pilot brought the ship into the berth and the coal was loaded by local Arab labour. It was carried in baskets on their heads and then they tipped it into the bunker hatches.

For the *Trevessa* it was a very brief stop and then on to Aden, another British colony. Here the ship stayed for a day moored on buoys and discharged mostly NAAFI stores for a British regiment stationed there at the time. These included the bullion, spirits, beer and foodstuffs.

Again the apprentices were engaged in watching this cargo and seeing it safely into the barges alongside. There, soldiers were on guard and the battle of wits to steal the cargo went on apace. In the holds it was not the bullion that was targeted, it was the foodstuffs, in particular the Dutch cheeses. The dockers were equipped with hand held hooks with which they pulled boxes and crates out of the cargo in the hold. They then lifted and placed the goods onto cargo trays to be lifted out of the ship. These hooks were also used to broach the boxes in an attempt to steal the contents. One or more of the men would distract the attention of the apprentices while this was going on. In most cases more than one had to be on watch, and the ship's officers gave a hand on this occasion.

Soon *Trevessa* was on her way once more, across the Indian Ocean to the port of Karachi in what was then Imperial India.

At sea the routine of watch keeping and weekly work was well established. The routine maintenance and running of the ship were paramount, with the two senior apprentices getting the choice of the tasks required of the boys.

A regular job for the four junior boys was to holystone the decks. This entailed pushing a square stone across the wooden decks, while they were on their knees. The two elder apprentices would hose down the deck first and keep it wet while the holystoning went on. They would also spread sand and broom this off after the operation, resulting in the deck gleaming white in the hot sun.

Chipping rust off the steel work, washing paint work, polishing brass work and oiling and greasing the ship's rigging and winch and derrick gear were all common week-day tasks.

On Saturday the cleaning of their accommodation was the main job during the morning and mending and patching their clothes during the afternoon. While on watch the boys would steer the ship, and the officer of the watch would ask questions on their knowledge of navigation and seamanship.

Sundays would see all the mattresses brought out on deck to air in the sun while the captain would make a long and thorough inspection of all the accommodation. Heaven help the apprentice whose cabin did not pass muster.

"It is quite clear to me that you need to work harder and so you will," he would say. "Extra watches for you, my lad. Then you will keep your cabin clean."

John stuck to his studies with determination. Because of his limited education he needed help and Douglas Bell obliged. They would study together both on watch and in their so-called spare time. Navigation in those days depended a good deal on logarithms – a kind of calculated table. These shortened the calculations in navigation and were vital to the navigator.

"Come on, I know you can do it. Now let's try again," Douglas would say as John would get an answer wrong.

"Oh, all right, I will," said John rubbing his eyes and struggling to stay awake. In seamanship it was the other way round, with John encouraging Douglas when he found it difficult.

On rare occasions an officer would help in cases where they were learning the use of the sextant in navigation, or checking their calculations. But for most of the time the boys had to help themselves and one can only wonder how they managed to master trigonometry, algebra, navigation, seamanship, signalling with flags and lights, amongst many other things. Yet both were to become skilled navigators and seamen in the years to come.

Karachi turned out hot, sticky and with an abundance of flies. This was a whole new experience for John, seeing a part of the British Empire at its imperial best. Although cargo discharge went on round the clock, the apprentices were able to get ashore to the seaman's mission, as they did in all the principal ports of India. Of course, they wore their tropical uniform and Captain Gibson gave them quite a lecture before going ashore for the first time.

"You are representatives of the British Merchant Navy," he said in his most imperious tone. "I expect you to wear your pith helmets while in the sun at all times. I expect you to be respectful to all Europeans and behave properly towards the Indians while you are ashore. If I hear of any trouble while you are ashore you will regret it for the rest of the time you are on this ship."

John was quite convinced he meant all of it. As a result he did not get into any scrapes ashore.

Here for the first time he observed the horse-drawn Garry (a type of wagonette) with an Indian driver carrying the ladies and gentlemen of the ruling power around the city. The ladies would carry their parasols to keep off the sun and talk in loud voices about their important friends. The men very often wore top hats and carried silver handled walking sticks or umbrellas. Sailors and Indians called these people 'Burra Sahibs'.

"These people have a rather high opinion of themselves," was John's reaction as he walked in the port for the first time. Certainly they looked down on mere ordinary members of the Merchant Navy; one had to be a 'Captain' to be welcome in their society. Soldiers stationed in the local garrison were regarded in much the same light. Of course Burra Sahibs carried out most of the well-paid jobs, leaving the menial tasks to Indians and others.

Small carriages called rickshaws and propelled by a man on a pedal cycle were everywhere, offering to take the apprentices to any destination. While on the streets the beggars thronged to get a gift from sailors ashore from their ship.

On board the *Trevessa* many Indian traders, and it must be said charlatans, attempted to sell and con money from the crew's pockets. Amongst those visiting were people offering tattoos, fortune telling, herbal medicines and so on. One such man persuaded one of the apprentices called Walter Courtney that he was suffering from an excess of wax in his ears.

"You see, Sahib, your hearing will be affected," the persuasive rogue said to the lad as he peered into his ear while he was sat in his cabin.

"Really?" said Walter. "Is it serious do you think?"

"Oh yes, you will be deaf in a couple of months at this rate of wax build up. Now look, Sahib, for just a rupee I will get rid of it in no time."

"OK," said the scared apprentice, "but I'm not paying you any more than a rupee."

"Right Sahib, just give me the money," the man said, and Walter did so.

At this point he then produced a dirty, semi-stiff rubber tube and sticking it into the lad's ears, sucked the wax out.

On hearing the story John always considered it a miracle that the lad did not have major ear trouble afterwards.

After Karachi it was on to Bombay and here the ship entered an enclosed dock for a much longer stay. The sailor's mission was one of the famous Flying Angel establishments run by a society with Church of England connections. Facilities were good, with games like billiards and table tennis and also cheap food. Here the boys could swim in a swimming pool and rest, and write letters away from the hot and noisy conditions on the ship. In fact it must have made quite an impression on John as he always supported Missions to Seaman throughout the rest of his life.

In Bombay John was to take part in a tradition carried out by most Cornish seaman wherever they went. On the docks he met a chief officer from St. Ives, serving with the British India Company on one of their coastal vessels trading around India. He was called Jennings and was based in Bombay for a three-year contract. He had married a St. Ives girl named Winnie Praed and they lived locally in Bombay. He was only too eager to meet and exchange news of home with John. So before leaving Bombay John took possession of a small gift for the immediate family back home in Cornwall.

Now it was on to Ceylon (now called Sri Lanka) and the port of Colombo. Here the ships moored on buoys in a large open harbour, and the ship's crews were not allowed ashore. Only the captain could visit Colombo and even then in the company of a customs officer or agent. Indeed, a customs officer stayed on board during the stay to keep track of the crew.

Nonetheless some relaxation was given to the apprentices in their free time. They were allowed to swim in the beautiful blue waters of the harbour and to board other company ships in port to chat to fellow apprentices and other acquaintances. In later years, John was to swim from one Hain vessel to another to see his pal Douglas Bell. On that occasion he took so long chatting that a Morse code message was flashed across the water telling him to await the arrival of the ship's lifeboat as it was getting dark. All too often in Colombo sharks swam into the port and the lads took turns to keep a lookout from the ship and warn the rest should there be any danger.

Large passenger liners called from time to time and all the crew looked on with envy as their passengers went ashore. By now the hot season was in full swing and with the sun beating down from cloudless skies, swimming was a real delight to the hard working crew of *Trevessa*. Much of the cargo for this port was sugar and it took some time to discharge, making the stay seem all too long for comfort.

After a week the ship sailed south and rounded Dondra Head, and then headed north into the Bay of Bengal. Proceeding at her stately eleven knots *Trevessa* arrived in Madras some two days later. Here the ship had a berth alongside, and the apprentices walked up to town and wandered around the market looking for possible presents for home. Sadly for John he did not have the money to spare and could only watch the others on these shopping expeditions. After the strict regulations of Colombo this port made for a complete change, but this visit lasted for only two days and then the ship headed northwards once again, towards the final port of discharge, Calcutta.

5

Calcutta

Some four days later the *Trevessa* approached the pilot station outside the Hooghly River and anchored to await a pilot. This area was known as Sandheads, with the only indication of land being the brown dirty water and the beautiful pilot cutter, which cruised around the ships at anchor. This vessel looked more like a very expensive yacht than a cutter and her bright paintwork and brass gleamed in the sun as she passed.

On board this vessel the British pilots lived a life of luxury, with comfortable accommodation, servants and fine food. There were two of these vessels and they each did a tour of three weeks before returning the 122 miles upriver to Calcutta.

After a two day wait John, together with two other apprentices, rigged a pilot ladder and stood by as the pilot launch brought the pilot over from the cutter. All three lads were needed to get him and his entourage on board. First came the pilot who was met by the second mate and conducted to the captain's cabin. Then the apprentices helped the pilot's cook with his pots and pans and food and showed him to his accommodation near the galley. Last but not least, the pilot's luggage (and there was plenty) had to be brought up to the pilot's cabin. While this was going on, the pilot was having a drink with the captain.

"We will get under way in about six hours, and I shall have a sleep first. My servant can use the time to unpack my things and make me a meal," he announced in a haughty voice.

Proceeding up the river was a tedious business and in all the passage took three days. At first all that was visible were the buoys marking the winding channel into the river mouth. Now and then a sandbank was visible but there was no sign of the land. Then, as the ship proceeded up the river, Indian villages, bushes and green fields teeming with people could be seen. On the river canoes and small sailing vessels and barges propelled by oars scurried out of the way of the approaching steamer.

At various times the pilot would announce that the vessel would be anchoring for a number of hours to await the next tide. John and the other apprentices would then help the mate and carpenter on the bow as the vessel made another of her stops.

During these times canoes would approach the ship to trade fruit and vegetables and the merchants would try to get aboard. The apprentices would be stationed on deck to prevent this happening with water hoses at the ready. On ships where these precautions were not taken, mooring ropes, paint and stores would all disappear very quickly. However, *Trevessa* was a well-run vessel and the strict discipline made sure that no such occurrence happened to her on passage up the river. Although it must be said that the hose was used on a couple of occasions to repel boarders.

At Calcutta a new experience was in store for the young apprentice, with the mooring of the vessel on buoys outside the dock system in the river. The Hooghly River suffers from huge bore tides, when a large wave followed by several small ones rushes up the waterway. These waves, combined with an eight-knot tide, are quite capable of parting all the moorings of a ship and special precautions have to be taken to ensure the vessels in the river do not break free.

On arrival all the crew were turned to at stations to moor the ship. After two ordinary ropes were made fast to the buoy, both forward and aft, the crew then removed both of the anchors from their chains. Then two lengths of chain were disconnected, each measuring thirty fathoms, and lowered to a barge under the bow, and these were then taken to the after buoy and joined to it by shackles. Then the other end of the chain was hauled by winch up to the poop and made fast on board. Meanwhile, at the bow, the two anchor chains were lowered by the windlass to the buoy at that end of the ship. These were then shackled on so that the vessel was moored with anchor chain at the bow and stern. Then special wires and tackles were placed on top of the chains just to make sure.

This involved a gruelling eight hours work on top of the normal watches that the boys had kept. Whilst moored in the river the crew would go to stations whenever a bore tide was due, usually over a three-day period every fourteen days or so. Occasionally one of the chains would break and a tug had to return with the barge, and the long recovery procedure would commence. An experience that many merchant seamen visiting the Hooghly River will remember.

Calcutta was one of the busiest ports in India, and to John it seemed there were hundreds of British vessels in the city. Outnumbering all other company ships were the black funnels with the two white bands around them signifying the British India Company. Also present were the vessels of the Brocklebank Line and P&O as well as many other British tramping ships. While on the buoys further up the river towards the imposing Howrah Bridge was a Royal Navy Cruiser. The British naval crew could be seen regularly ashore in the markets and parks in their tropical rig.

In Calcutta there was a British garrison and John watched with wonder as the troops could be seen marching to church on Sunday mornings, while in the afternoon he enjoyed the military bands giving recitals in the Midan Park. Naturally the Burra Sahibs, with their ladies attending in their carriages, took no notice of John or his companions.

Meanwhile the crew on the ship engaged in night work were able to sleep in the mission, which indeed was a privilege. One of the hazards of the port was the presence of millions of mosquitoes with the threat of malaria, whereas at the mission there was a plentiful supply of mosquito netting in the cool airy rooms. In Calcutta itself many hundreds were dying each day from cholera, and this was not unusual in those times.

After three weeks *Trevessa* shifted from the river into the Kiddepore dock behind lock gates. All the moorings had been recovered and the anchors reconnected – another eight-hour task. Then as the discharge ended, the captain would go ashore each day and visit the agents to await his sailing orders. Each evening, as he returned, the chief officer would meet Captain Gibson.

"Are there any orders, Captain?" he would say, wanting to know what the next employment of the ship was to be.

"I will let you know when *I* know, Mr Williams," would be the grumpy reply as the captain made for his cabin. Eventually, after an eight-day wait with the ship empty, they had to move out into the river once more. They moored two miles down the waterway on to buoys with all the same precautions as before. These proved very necessary, as the ship was to wait a further six weeks for a cargo.

During this time the captain would go ashore each day (except Sundays) in a company canoe to obtain orders. Mail, of course, came by sea to India and the captain would collect any from the agents, all of which had taken at least seven weeks to arrive.

One event of note did occur during this period. Early one morning the brand new German vessel *Sternfels* arrived in Calcutta. This caused some wry comments from the crew as the *Trevessa* had, as the *Imkenturm,* belonged to the same German company. Mutters of "Who won the war?" could be heard as the crew stopped work to observe this ship. Her clean paintwork and modern looking accommodation caused a great deal of envy as she passed by.

During this time Indian labour had been employed to chip and paint the ship's sides, while the crew, with the apprentices now working days, toiled at making the decks and accommodation spotless. Also the holds of the ship were washed and painted and prepared for cargo. The apprentices were taught by the seamen to splice and make cargo slings and to prepare the ship's running wires and ropes for loading.

As the days passed Captain Gibson's return each day was eagerly awaited. A little group of officers would meet him at the

41

gangway, while crew and apprentices would wait close by to hear the latest news.

Eventually the awaited day came, and Captain Gibson was heard to say to the chief engineer, "Raise steam tomorrow Chief, we will be on our way in two days." Then, turning to Mr Williams, "Is that what you wanted to hear, Mr Mate? We shall be bound for Rangoon in Burma to load a full cargo of rice for Hamburg in Germany." As he spoke he was surprised at the reaction of the crew who raised a loud cheer. They were indeed fed up with their long stay on the river and eager to be on their way. So it was with a will that the crew began the task of dismantling the moorings and preparing for sea.

Before the passage down the river the ship's double bottom tanks were filled with river-water as ballast. Careful note was made of the remaining coal for bunkers and calculations made of how far the ship could proceed before needing more. These were made all the more difficult as the vessel would be heading into the south-west monsoon season in coming days. All storerooms had to be checked and the all-movable stores secured against heavy weather. So it was a busy time before the ship dropped her pilot at Sandheads and made the three-day journey to Rangoon.

That port was twenty-three miles up the Irrawady River, and on arrival the vessel had once more to go through the long process of making fast to buoys with the anchor chains. Here a surveyor now checked the gleaming holds and gave orders for all the bare steel in these spaces to be covered with a form of rush mat. Also delivered to the ship were wooden ventilators consisting of rough wood made into the form of a framework like a wooden pipe. These were stacked in each hold by the apprentices, ready for use as the loading proceeded.

Then barges full of bagged rice were towed alongside and loading began. In carrying such a cargo great care was needed both in loading and transporting the rice. At various intervals during the loading the framework ventilators intersected bags both horizontally and vertically. These then led up to the ship's permanent hold ventilators in which thermometers were hung to check the temperature. Attached to a light line these could be checked during the sea voyage.

Care had to be taken not to rest any bag against the cold steel of the ship. Otherwise the bagged rice would sweat, and in producing this moisture could ruin the cargo or even catch fire with spontaneous combustion. The mates and senior apprentices kept a special watch over the stowing of the cargo, making sure that the rows of bags were in good order. Also they would watch the weather because rain could have the same effect as sweating. As soon as rain threatened, the hold would be covered over and loading cease.

Ashore, the sight of the gold covered Pagoda that dominated the waterfront impressed John a great deal and he visited the temple with some of his shipmates. It gleamed in the sunshine and the boys much enjoyed seeing the various processions making their way there.

Then followed the long voyage back to Germany. After the discharge of the cargo in September the *Trevessa* paid a short visit to South Shields, once more to dry dock and check her hull plating. John did not have the money to return home so he stayed with the ship over this period. His working clothes were well worn by this time and he was forced to write to his long-suffering father in St. Ives asking for money to replace them. He received six pounds in a registered letter and this allowed him, under the supervision of the chief officer, to buy fresh gear for the next trip. The *Trevessa* then loaded a full cargo of coal for Colombo and with some new crew on board set sail once more for Ceylon.

Then the ship was to trade mainly around the Indian Ocean with coal and other tramping cargoes for the next sixteen months, although she did make one voyage to China in August 1921. Typical of voyages was a cargo of 6,480 tons of coal taken from Deligo Bay, in Portuguese East Africa, to Madras, on the east coast of India, in May 1922. Records kept at St. Ives show that the owners received on average about £7,000 per cargo, or to put it another way, about twenty-one shillings and sixpence per ton carried.

During this period Douglas Bell was landed at Colombo in February 1922 with malaria, rejoining the ship in Rangoon in

March of that year, five weeks later. It had been a serious illness but he must have recovered well, as he was to be one of the survivors after the ship sank in the Indian Ocean in 1923.

On the Indian Coast the vessel sailed throughout two south-west monsoon seasons, usually well loaded and low in the water. Following his retirement John himself described these times of bad weather and his apprehensions as he made his way round the decks.

"She did not cope very well with bad weather when fully loaded," he said. "She shipped a lot of seawater and laboured very heavily in the monsoon swell conditions. There were times when I was on the deck when I really feared for my safety. It almost seemed that the ship dipped into the swell encouraging the sea to come aboard." However he kept his doubts to himself and worked hard at his studies.

October of 1922 was to find *Trevessa* loading in India with a general cargo for Genoa, Antwerp, Leith and Liverpool.

At this time John was to come to a fateful decision: that he would leave the *Trevessa* after her homeward voyage. This was rather more difficult than it seemed, as Captain Gibson considered that all apprentices should complete their apprentice-ship time of four years on one ship. Indeed he had declared openly within the crew's hearing that, "Apprentices leaving before their indentured time reflected badly on the ship." Therefore any apprentice wishing to leave got short shrift from him and probably a bad report as well. No consideration was given to the experience of the apprentice concerned, only the reputation of the ship.

So John did not tell Captain Gibson. He wrote to the company direct, asking for a transfer to another vessel. With the slow speed of mail it was in Genoa that the now furious master found out about this request. His reaction to a first trip apprentice telling him that he did not like the sea-keeping qualities of his vessel was a bout of real fury.

"How dare you," he thundered, "tell me that this fine ship is not to your liking? What do you know about it anyway? You will withdraw this request at once."

Now all the ill-treatment at home in his younger years came to John's aid. In a quiet but defiant voice he refused to budge. He had little to say, he just kept shaking his head and saying, "No, I will not."

The rest of the voyage was a nightmare for John, with every dirty job and duty being assigned to apprentice Kemp. Nevertheless, John stuck to his point of view and none of the pressure would induce him to change it. While on watch one evening when the ship was crossing the Bay of Biscay the third officer, John Daniel, took John aside.

"Now look here John," he said in a lowered voice. "I really think you should come back next voyage. The captain is really up tight about it. He will give you a bad report and the company will not be pleased when you get back home."

It all had no affect on John, not even the pleading of his mate Douglas Bell.

"Come on John," he said, "stay with us next trip. You know the skipper is leaving anyway."

"No," said John, "I do not feel safe on this ship and I am not rejoining her. You do as you please Doug, I'm not coming back."

At Genoa he spent ten shillings, for him a fortune, to buy a painting of the *Trevessa* entering the port. His shore leave was cancelled as a punishment for his defiance of Captain Gibson's wishes, but the artist came on board to sell the painting. This picture was to hang in his home to his dying day. Now it resides in the St. Ives Museum as a part of their excellent Hain Room.

John left the ship in Liverpool, after discharging in Continental ports before her departure for Canada. Here he was to bid farewell to the other apprentices, including Douglas Bell. He also met his relief, Harry Sparks, a new apprentice from Lelant near St. Ives.

6

Drifting for Sixty Days

Back in St. Ives, John faced the disapproving face of Mr Cogar as he reported to the company office. "So, Master Kemp, you are not satisfied with the *Trevessa* then?" said the company secretary. "Well I must say the directors are most annoyed, they do not like bad reports about their apprentices. You will be joining one of our older vessels and I advise you to do better in future."

After a short leave he joined the 3,075 gross ton *Tregothnan,* built in 1903 at the Redhead Yard in South Shields. This four-hatch ship was a classic solid British tramp of her day. Simple and sturdy in every way, would be a good description of the vessel. Built to last, she was still trading for Turkish owners some fifty-eight years later. However, the comfort of the crew was one of the last considerations in her planning. All four apprentices lived in one cabin that was so small that only one could dress at a time. Quite a problem when they were wanted for an urgent job on deck. In fact the company had difficulty in getting good crews for this vessel due to the very basic conditions on board. So John found himself on a ship with limited fresh water supplies, a troublesome crew and poor accommodation.

Trevessa, now under the command of Captain Foster, was in Saint John in New Brunswick, Canada, loading for New Zealand and Australia.

Meanwhile the old *Tregothnan* was loading just over six

thousand tons of good Welsh steam coal at Swansea. Young Kemp had to buckle down to his new ship and make the best of it.

In fact, right from the beginning of the trip, the water had to be rationed, with just one wash a day for the crew. During rainstorms at sea the boys would put out any pot or pan they could get to collect fresh water. It was only the fact that the ship was running constantly to South America from South Wales that kept any regular crew on board.

So at the stately speed of seven and a half knots the ship set out for the River Plate. All went well on the outward voyage and in due course, some six weeks later, the ship commenced discharge of her cargo in Buenos Aires.

Ashore during this time a revolution was brewing in true Argentinean style and a change of Government was due. Following the discharge of the coal cargo the ship was to proceed upriver to the port of Rosario to load wheat for Antwerp in Belgium. The problem was that no one knew what conditions would be like under a new government, and there was the possibility that the ship could be caught up in the fighting if she proceeded up the river, so instead she headed out into the South Atlantic to await developments.

Once clear of the land all engines were shut down to conserve fuel, and food and water were strictly rationed. Just one oil lamp was allowed in the apprentice's accommodation and that only for moving about at night when it was necessary.

One good effect of this enforced stoppage was that after the holds were prepared for grain the officers had plenty of time on their hands. This meant they regularly called the apprentices to the bridge and tested them on their knowledge of seamanship and navigation. Signalling practice by semaphore flags and Morse lamp was regularly carried out between apprentices on the fo'c'sle, the bridge and the poop aft. Messages sent from the fo'c'sle were checked at the poop and woe betide the apprentices if they were not relayed correctly.

Tregothnan waited for sixty days before receiving the order to proceed, and nearly all the food and water had gone by the time the ship made her way up the river to load. Not to mention that the crew were in a really mutinous mood before the orders arrived. Then with a full cargo of grain they were off just a week later for Antwerp and home.

Following this discharge in June of 1923, *Tregothnan* was ordered to proceed to Falmouth for a refit and dry-docking. During the stay in Cornwall she was sold to the F. C. Strick line. They modernised the vessel and used her on their Persian Gulf trade until 1928 when she was sold once more to Egyptian owners.

On arrival off Falmouth in June 1923, the pilot brought dramatic news to John as he stood at the top of the pilot ladder. "Have you heard," he said as he stepped on to the deck, "the *Trevessa*, carrying a full cargo of zinc concentrates from Port Pirie in Australia, has foundered somewhere in the Indian Ocean and the crew are missing?"

It was to be some time before the news arrived of the epic voyage in two lifeboats by the crew of *Trevessa*, ending successfully in Mauritius and Rodrigues. One boat had travelled seventeen hundred miles and the other twenty-two hundred miles.

Sadly, the relief apprentice Harry Sparks had died with several others in the open lifeboats on the voyage. Happily, Douglas Bell was to be one of the survivors.

Much publicity followed the return of the crew to the United Kingdom, but no one outside the company found out that a young apprentice had refused to sail in the ship on that fateful voyage. Now there was a completely new attitude to this young apprentice from his superiors. Firstly a smile from the company superintendent when he boarded at Falmouth: "You can go home on leave, my boy, for a couple of days," he said. Then an interview followed with the managers of the company at St. Ives.

"You have done really well and we are very pleased with you young Kemp," said Mr Cogar. He made no mention of John leaving the *Trevessa*, and John never raised the subject. No doubt satisfied that he was not going to cause trouble they appointed him as senior apprentice to the SS *Trebartha*, then in London.

The SS *Trebartha*, 4,597 gross tons, had only been completed

Lifeboat drill in the Indian Ocean on SS *Burdwan*.

Officers on the SS *Burdwan* celebrate Jubilee Day at sea in 1935.

Cargo being loaded at Port Sweetham, Malaya, on the
SS *Burdwan*, Christmas 1935.

John Kemp, new chief mate of the
SS *Teviotbank* in 1939.

SS *Teviotbank* in New Zealand before her war service.

John Kemp's son Eric – another prospective
mariner visiting SS *Teviotbank*.

Now HMS *Teviotbank*, with Lieutenant John Kemp RNR,
on passage to lay mines in the North Sea, 1940.

Mines delivered to Immingham Docks by rail in1941.

Lieutenant Kemp in charge of operations on the
mine-laying deck of HMS *Teviotbank*.

Captain, officers and crew – HMS *Teviotbank*, 1941.

HMS *Teviotbank*
at anchor,
Invergordon.

HMS *Teviotbank*
in Convoy, 1941.
Escorting warship
turns to investi-
gate sighting of a
German E boat.

Convoy protection
for HMS *Teviotbank*

The coastal vessel *PLM 14* suffering bomb damage.
Picture taken from HMS *Teviotbank*.

On board HMS *Teviotbank* the crew paint a picture of
Hitler on the 10,000th mine laid.

in 1920. A five-hatch ship, she carried six apprentices. They slept in double berth cabins and had their own mess-room and lived in reasonably comfortable conditions. The ship was under the command of a Captain Symons, and on this vessel John was to complete his apprenticeship trading in the Indian Ocean, Australia and Europe. Here he was to have his first experience of the copra cargoes with all the bugs that went with them. Also he was to observe the ship load a full cargo of zinc concentrates at Port Pirie for the continent just as the *Trevessa* had two years before.

Although the ship went to Rotterdam and Antwerp during this time she did not arrive back into Great Britain until August 1925. John had now served his apprenticeship time and on the 9th of January 1925 was signed on the vessel at sea as an able seaman, with a princely wage of eight pounds per month. He then served in this capacity until 23rd of August 1925, when the ship had finally docked at Falmouth for a refit once more.

It is interesting to read the reference given to John by Captain Symons on that date. It reads: 'This is to certify that the bearer Mr J. Kemp has served on the above vessel as an apprentice and AB from July 22nd 1923 until August 23rd 1925 completing his indentures at sea. I have at all times found him a willing and obedient "Young Man" being attentive to his various duties and strictly sober in his habits.' Maybe he should have shown that reference to the headmaster at the St. Ives school who predicted he was only a troublemaker.

It was only the first of many such references as he rose in rank in the British Merchant Navy. Now it was a case of going to school and passing his second mate's examination, then getting back to sea to continue his career.

That year of 1925 had seen Winston Churchill put Great Britain back on the gold standard. As a result the pound had risen in value against other currencies and much of Britain's exports were becoming very expensive. As John came back to St. Ives, the local newspaper was forecasting a difficult winter with many people out of work.

John did not take too much notice at first. After a short leave he enrolled at the sea school in Plymouth and worked and studied

e

hard to obtain his second mate's certificate. By Christmas it was in his pocket and he returned home confident of getting a berth once more with Hain's.

At the office he was in for a shock. Due to the employment situation many officers were staying with their ships. The company always had more apprentices than it could use, and in January 1926 all it could offer John was to place his name on a waiting list. Over the next five months he was to try many companies but with ships laying up and looming industrial troubles, culminating in the general strike during May, he could get no work.

During this time the young eligible sailor walked out with a number of local girls. Over the months he decided that he favoured Ann Uren. She was now a dark-haired, beautiful young woman taking a full part in worship at the Primitive Chapel in the town. Ann had four elder sisters and one brother and was very much the apple of her father's eye. In order to walk out with Ann, John had to attend the chapel services. At much the same time he had also kept company with some of the other girls. His method of revealing his regular girlfriend was quite unique, and was not really appreciated by the young lady concerned.

"Coming out for a walk tonight, Ann?"

"Yes, of course," said Ann.

"Right, we will make the rounds of the town then. See you after tea."

What he had not told her was that at various points around the locality he had also invited other girls to meet him for a date. These young ladies were far too polite or disgusted to say anything as the pair passed. Ann could not understand the black looks she was receiving from some of her friends. Eventually she commented on the fact, as the sixth friend cut her dead as they passed.

"I don't understand why I'm getting so many black looks," she told John.

"I do," said John. "I wanted to show them all that I had chosen you as my regular girl, so I arranged to meet all of them for a date tonight."

Ann was flabbergasted. "How dare you do this to me?" she stormed, but John had made a hit and she came to see the compliment he had paid her.

Of course, Ann had to be home by 10 o'clock in the evening, even though she was in her twenties. Her father was a fisherman and local preacher in the Fore Street Methodist Chapel. (One wonders what he thought of his youngest and favourite daughter courting this seaman who, even in those days, liked a pint of beer when he was ashore.)

By June 1926 the general strike had collapsed and John was running out of money. He was unable to get an officer's berth and so reluctantly signed on the P & O passenger liner SS *Novara*, 4,249 net tons, as quartermaster.

Running on the Calcutta Service, each voyage took three months and John completed two such trips before leaving the vessel in January 1927. This appointment was with the agreement of the Hain Steamship Company as they had vessels laid up at the time.

These voyages gave him his first experience of dealing with Indian crews. He had to keep a constant watch, at sea on the bridge and in port on the gangway, acting as a sort of ship's policeman.

In February 1927 he at last got a berth as third officer in the SS *Trevean*, 5,225 gross tons. This vessel had been ordered by the Government in 1918 as the SS *War Quail* and with the end of the war had been completed as cheaply as possible. She was regarded as a reliable workhorse by the company and served the company well until 1931. Under Captain M. E. Sadler she was a happy ship and John completed four voyages in her without leave, finishing in August 1928 at Barry in South Wales.

Then a period at Plymouth followed, and he obtained his first mate's certificate in just ten weeks. He was still going steady with Ann and she had agreed to wait until he had obtained his Master's ticket before they would marry.

Now his reputation was rising in the company and he joined the brand new cargo liner SS *Bangalore*, 6,067 gross tons, as third officer in Middlesbrough. This vessel, with four others, had been specially ordered for the P & O Company. They were manned by Hain's men and ran on a special service at 15 knots to India, China and Japan, calling at forty-two ports every three months. These ships were popular amongst the Hain crews as they worked regular voyages from London in the general cargo trade. However, to keep to a very strict schedule demanded long hours of hard work by all the crews. John was to stay eighteen months in the ship completing six voyages.

In August 1928 he was promoted second officer, and despite the long hours of work he studied hard to get his Master's Certificate.

During this time the great stock market crash occurred, and keeping your job became a real concern. One effect on the *Bangalore* was that officers were expected to look after domestic pets and other animals being transported to their owners in India and other parts of the Empire. Naturally horses and other large animals were carried in proper stalls in the holds. Smaller pets, however, fared better travelling in the officers' cabins.

On one such trip, in December 1929, John had to care for a very lively spaniel. On coming off watch at four in the morning, while crossing the Bay of Biscay and with the ship rolling heavily, the dog got out of John's cabin as he was entering. To John's horror the animal dashed straight out on to the deck and fell overboard.

After breakfast John then had to face Captain Thomas Kemp with the very awkward news that the dog was lost overboard. The master, a canny gentleman by all accounts, gave John the dressing down of his life. He then made the young second officer go and get the ship's official logbook from the bridge. There he wrote that the dog had developed a slight temperature, he then handed the book over to the young second mate to sign. This little meeting occurred for the next seven days as the vessel proceeded into warmer waters. Each day the dog's condition worsened and eventually the dog's death and burial at sea were recorded in the book. After all, if the truth were known, the captain was quite likely to lose his job as well.

Despite this incident John progressed well on the *Bangalore*, and he left the ship when she docked at Falmouth on the 29th of June 1930, with a good reference.

By August he was back at school in Plymouth, and in October he had passed as a Master Mariner. This was truly a great achievement for the young man, in many ways a tribute to his mother who had so stoutly declared many years before, "He'll learn."

Now back home in St. Ives, the newly qualified Master Mariner faced the great slump and a long wait to get work. John and Ann had delayed their wedding until better times came along. In the meantime Ann worked in a local net factory mending nets to make some money towards her wedding day.

Five and half months were to pass before John was to get work again. He would wait with others outside Hain's Office in the town to see if any work was forthcoming. Following these gatherings, occasionally the young unemployed mariners would meet at the Queens Hotel for a pint, where they discussed some of their problems.

At this time John's brother Sam was home from his job in the China Customs Service. He used to join the party and, being in the Colonial Service and thus well off, provided quite a lot of the beer.

On one occasion, in 1931, a local seaman was amongst those at the pub. He was due to join a coaster sailing that day from Portreath, a small port to the east of St. Ives bay. This man quite forgot the time, and in a very jolly mood suddenly realised that he had missed the transport from St. Ives to Portreath.

Now Sam was the proud owner of a Morris Tourer. This car had an outside brake and gear change and was the pride of his life. Being the heart and soul of the party he agreed to take the sailor to Portreath to catch the ship. John and three of his mates also went along for the ride. All went well until the car containing the jolly party came down the steep hill into the very small harbour. Half way down the hill, to the great alarm of Sam, the brakes ceased to work. Somehow the vehicle got round the hairpin turn in the road and sped on to the tiny harbourside. To stop they had to run into a huge pile of coal.

Not in the least disturbed the sailor alighted from the damaged car. "Thank you, my friend," he said solemnly, and with rolling gate boarded his ship. He was just in time because the crew were in the act of letting the ropes go and leaving for sea.

Sam was almost at a loss for words, all five had to struggle to straighten the bent bumper and engine grill. It was very late before the lads got home that night, nursing Sam's damaged car.

7

The Great Slump

At last a job did become available and in mid-April 1931 John joined the SS *Trelawny*, 4,689 gross tons, as second mate. This ship had been built at the Hawthorn Leslie yard on the Tyne and was completed in 1927. Her crew had been cut in number and she only carried two mates. So it was watch and watch again for John, just like his days on the *Trevessa*.

He was to make six voyages on the vessel, all to the River Plate, with coal on the outward journey and wheat on the homeward passage.

On his first voyage an incident was to occur which clearly showed the value of a cool head in a dangerous situation. As the vessel went up the river before loading wheat, a Dutch vessel named SS *Ameland* approached them proceeding down the river fully loaded. They were due to pass one another on the Montiel bend.

Captain Devereux was below and John was on watch with the river pilot. As the other ship entered the bend her steering gear failed and she sailed straight on at the port side of the oncoming *Trelawney*. On the bridge of the Hain vessel the pilot began shouting at the oncoming vessel in Spanish to no effect. John quickly realised that as things were developing the other ship would run straight into his ship's engine room, with disastrous consequences for those down below as well as the ship herself.

"Hard a port," he yelled at the helmsman. Luckily the sailor on the wheel obeyed at once and the bow of the *Trelawney* swung towards the oncoming Dutchman. As a result the Dutch vessel collided with number four hatch at a lesser angle, doing considerable damage. But the ship stayed afloat and managed to come clear of the other vessel. Without that order the engine room could have filled with water and the ship sunk there in the channel.

After some temporary repairs the ship then had to await a fresh charter before loading, and then proceeded to the Continent with another cargo of grain. On completion of discharge in Genoa she then went on to Falmouth for dry docking and repair.

As a reward for his actions John was to spend a month in Falmouth acting as chief officer during this period. Every officer except the chief engineer and John were paid off while the vessel was in the port. Every day the ship would be visited by the marine superintendent and all on board had to justify their continued employment. However the gentleman normally did not appear over the weekend.

So taking a big chance, on the 1st of August 1931, with the aid of a special licence, John married Ann Uren at the Parade Street Methodist Chapel, Penzance. All through the ceremony he had to worry about the superintendent turning up on the ship in Falmouth. Had he done so, John would have lost his job, but all was well and the bride and groom departed for their honeymoon on the *Trelawny* in dry dock. On the Sunday the happy couple had a river trip up the Fal to Truro, but during working days Ann either spent her time in Falmouth or hiding in the second mate's cabin.

Sadly though, during his eighteen months of service on the ship, tragedy was to strike the newly married couple. Ann gave birth to a little girl who died within a few hours. John at that time was berthed in Barry and requested a two day leave to go home and see his wife. The marine superintendent's remarks on receiving the request were typical of the time but they left a burning resentment with John.

"There are thirty second mates waiting for a job right now in the town, go home and you will not come back," he said.

So, bitterly disappointed, he stayed for one more voyage and left the vessel in November 1932, and was forced to live for five months with his in-laws at St. Ives while he waited for another job.

Then, in April 1933, he was appointed to the SS *Burdwan* under Captain E. Daniel from Falmouth. This 6,067 gross ton vessel was a sister ship to the *Bangalore* and was also engaged in the same high-speed service to India, China and Japan. Altogether he was to serve three and a half years in the ship without leave. Unthinkable today, but in those days it was taken for granted.

In September 1936, after two voyages as chief officer, the company announced a fleet reduction and offered John the second mate's job on the ship. He refused, and came home to St. Ives to face an uncertain future. Ann was soon pregnant and John resolved to stay with his wife until the baby was born.

Together they moved to Romford in Essex and took lodgings there. He got a job on the production line at Ford's Dagenham factory and Ann came under the care of the local hospital in Romford. This was one of the best at that time and John had resolved there would be no slip-up with this pregnancy.

June 1937 proved a happy time, when on the 29th their son Eric was safely born. By 1938 John had returned to sea and he served for short periods in the SS *Lahore,* 5,252 gross tons, and the 6,677 gross ton SS *Soudan*, as chief officer.

At this time job prospects were improving and John had not forgotten his treatment by the Hain Company when his daughter had died. So in December 1938, during some Christmas leave, he told Ann that he was going to find a new shipping line to serve. One company that was advertising for officers was Andrew Weir.

It is interesting to read John's reference from the Hain Line. It gives a full description of his officers' appointments and admits that due to reduction in their ship numbers they would not be able to promote him in the near future. They wished him well and commended him to any future employer.

Andrew Weir, or the Bank Line as they were known, were a Scottish Company and had been in existence since 1885. In that year Andrew Weir from Kirkcaldy bought his first sailing ship, the iron barque *Willowbank* of 882 gross tons. They went on owning sailing vessels until after the First World War, but also bought steamers and oil tankers in the early days of their development. During the world slump in the early nineteen thirties (in contrast to Hain's who had twelve ships laid up in the River Fal) Bank Line kept all its vessels at sea. They also built new ships in this period, putting them in a better position than most to take advantage of the upturn in world trade.

With over fifty ships trading world wide they were an important player in the tramp ship trades. Captain Howie, their marine superintendent, was impressed at the young officer he interviewed, and late in January 1939 he was able to offer John an appointment on the SS *Teviotbank,* 5,087 gross tons, as chief officer.

John joined the vessel which was then lying at the Woolwich buoys in the London River. This ship had been built at the John Redhead yard on the River Tyne and had only just completed her maiden voyage. She had a speed of eleven knots developed from her triple expansion steam engine. On his first voyage the captain, like many in the Bank Line at that time, was a canny Scotsman, John Tullock. John soon settled into the routine as chief officer and was well pleased with both his new appointment and his new shipmates.

Leaving the London River they proceeded to Flushing for coal, and then made a ballast voyage to Aden. There the ship loaded a full cargo of salt for Japan. Then followed a ballast voyage to Nauru, in the Pacific, to load phosphates for New Plymouth in New Zealand. Sydney, Australia, was the next port, to load wheat destined for Glasgow. After bunkering at Port Kembla, sixty miles from Sydney, the ship set off for Durban. But the weather took a hand on the long voyage to South Africa, with prolonged westerly gales reducing the speed of the ship. This must have reminded John of the last voyage of the *Trevessa* some sixteen years before. During the last few days of the voyage the coal bunkers began to run low, and the prospect of not making Durban loomed. This caused great friction between the chief engineer and the captain.

"I am sorry," the chief engineer Mr Sinclair remarked. "You wanted to get a move on at the last port, Captain, when we were bunkering, so I couldn't get as much coal as I needed."

"Nonsense," shouted the skipper, "you did not tell me you wanted more coal."

Fortunately John had not forgotten waiting for sixty days off the River Plate in the *Tregothnan*, and he had saved all the rough wood and spare timber from the last cargo. Now all the crew, including the cook, turned to with saws, and working in relays they fed the stokehold boilers for three days. As a result the ship arrived at Durban with just fifteen tons of coal left. This proved enough to manoeuvre the ship alongside the coaling berth. At which point the captain and the chief engineer were not on speaking terms and John was forced to be their 'go between' for the next few days.

Meanwhile the clouds of war were gathering all through 1938 and into 1939. By February of 1939 the Germans had launched the pocket battleship *Bismark* and Anderson shelters were being developed to protect people against the bombing of British homes. At last the government was waking up to the likelihood of war and recruiting for the forces was in full swing. Following the discharge of the wheat cargo, *Teviotbank* sailed to Huelva in Spain and loaded iron pyrites for Baltimore, sailing from there on the first of September 1939.

On the third of September John sat with the captain and the chief engineer to hear the declaration of war on the master's private radio. During the voyage secret orders were opened, and the vessel began zigzag courses during the day and direct courses at night to Baltimore. The crew painted the ship grey and prepared and tested the blackout. Following discharge, instead of loading the usual general cargo for Australia, the ship proceeded to Philadelphia. There a full cargo of pig iron was loaded for Glasgow in record time.

The voyage across the Atlantic was hazardous, with German raiders at sea and U-boats an ever present menace. However, luck and good fortune (which was never to desert the freighter) was with the *Teviotbank*, and by the 24th of October John's wife Ann and son Eric had joined him aboard the ship at Glasgow.

For some unknown reason Ann dressed Eric all in white and he very quickly showed the same naughty traits as his father many years before. As John got on with the work of discharging the cargo of pig iron, Eric slipped his mother's care and disappeared from his cabin. Shortly after, all hands on board the ship were searching for a little boy who could have fallen to his death in a dozen different places. He had actually got on to the boat-deck and crept into the nearly full coal-bunker hatch. There, with his white clothes soiled beyond recognition, he was throwing pieces of coal out on to the deck. His mother got quite a rocket over that one and made really sure that Eric did not wander again.

The next day the third mate, a Mr Broadley, agreed to baby-sit while John and Ann went ashore for a meal and to visit a cinema. On getting back a little early John found a party of officers surrounding his little lad in the cabin. They were offering him sips out of their beer bottles and laughing as he made faces and was saying, "I don't like these drinks they are too bitter."

All too soon these pranks were to end and those on board were to get a real shock. Unbeknown to them then, all the officers faced a very different future.

8

A Naval Officer
on HMS *Teviotbank*

At sea the loss of British shipping was mounting. HMS *Courageous* had been lost with 500 hands and merchant shipping was paying a terrible price for being unprepared for war.

While the cargo was being discharged, John watched a group of men moving around the decks in the company of Captain Tullock. Although dressed in civilian clothes their bearing was military. Amongst the group was a man John recognised; Commander R. D. King Harman, a former senior ship's pilot from the port of Singapore. As the group passed John on the deck, Commander Harman stopped to talk to him.

"I suppose," he started, "you are wondering what I am doing here."

John agreed.

"Well," said the Commander RNR, "the navy are taking this vessel over to be a mine-layer and I am to be the new captain. I would like you to stay with the ship and accept a commission as a Lieutenant RNR. Anyway, your company directors will board shortly and you will have a few days to decide."

Next day, after a talk with Ann, John agreed to join the Royal Navy Reserve. In fact all the officers did likewise at the special request of the owner of the Bank Line, Lord Inverforth.

Over the next two months the *Teviotbank* began the conversion to a mine-layer at Denny's yard in Dumbarton. Her 'tween-decks were turned into a mine deck with four sets of railway lines. These started in the old number one hatch near the bow and ran towards the stern where they merged into two. On the stern two watertight doors were fitted and through these the mines would be laid. In the centre of the deck various compartments were constructed to store the primers and detonators for the mines. While amidships the top of the engine room formed a part of this complex. All in all it looked and felt rather like an underground railway station.

During this period the Indian crew had left the vessel to return to Calcutta and new Royal Navy officers and ratings joined. Throughout, John worked and was in charge of this mine-laying deck and this was to be his action station until his promotion to Lieutenant Commander and second in command of the ship in 1942.

Meanwhile, on the home front, John's wife Ann and his son Eric returned to Romford in October and later moved back to their home-town of St. Ives.

By Christmas 1939 the basic changes to the ship had been completed and on the 27th of December seventy ratings arrived from Chatham to make up the crew of one hundred and eight men. Their ages ranged from eighteen to twenty-one and they had very little experience of the sea, let alone the Royal Navy.

So it was a 'very green crew' that took the ship down the River Clyde. In the Firth they carried out engine trials and compass adjustment prior to their first voyage under the white ensign to Portsmouth in January 1940. Now as HMS *Teviotbank,* the ship set off on her first naval passage in very similar weather conditions as that experienced on the SS *Trevessa* on John's first trip to sea. It was very cold, with a north-west gale and snow showers.

The newly converted mine-layer rolled and pitched in the seaway very violently indeed. Buckets and tin gear slid across the mess decks as the young crew learned the necessity to lash their gear down at sea. In most cases that was academic anyway as the newcomers were violently seasick, just as John's companions in the *Trevessa* had been all those years before.

Indeed, for them the first part of the voyage was a nightmare. The wind rattling in the rigging and searching out any gap in defences against the cold. The constant smell of sickness and the physical effort of balancing against the motion of the ship made it a very tough baptism for these new recruits to the Royal Navy. Due to the very heavy weather the ship sheltered at Milford Haven and here the old salts among the crew were able to really press home to the new men some of the practical skills of good sailors. It is fair to say that when the ship left Milford Haven she was in a better shape than previously.

The voyage around the west country proved easier and eventually the ship berthed in Portsmouth to continue her preparations to go to war. Here various tradesmen completed the transformation to a naval ship of war. Cork chippings were applied to the mess deck bulkheads to minimise excessive condensation. Emergency escape hatches were installed to serve the newly built accommodation. A twelve-pounder gun was mounted on the poop with two Lewis guns on either side of the bridge.

Training runs were carried out off the Isle of Wight, in which dummy mines were handled on the mining deck to get some idea of the tasks to come. All the time the ex-Merchant Navy men had to learn the Royal Navy way of doing things. In these early days John did find himself in hot water for being too familiar with his men. However, his practical knowledge of the ship and skill in moving mines and gear, insured he did not suffer too much at this early stage.

In 1940 the IRA had started a bombing campaign in Birmingham and posters everywhere cautioned people to be careful with their words. One such poster showed a sinking merchant vessel torpedoed by a U-boat and the caption read 'Careless words cost lives'. So as January passed and February came, worried speculation as to the destination of the *Teviotbank* increased. Captain Tullock, the navigating officer, now left the ship to be replaced by a regular naval officer, as departure time neared.

Eventually the ship sailed from Portsmouth and headed east up the Channel. Now with a crew of a hundred and twenty-three and the guns manned for action she sailed in a small coastal convoy through the Straits of Dover and then northwards up the east coast.

Although this time was called the 'phoney war', the crew could see many wrecks testifying to the reality of the situation in these confined waters. Strong easterly winds did not help on the passage and seasickness again ravaged the crew. But the men were now becoming a much better team and the routine of the warship at sea was not disrupted by the weather. Eventually the final destination turned out to be Immingham. Here in the very early hours of a cold February morning, the *Teviotbank* locked into the dock system and berthed alongside to bunker and load her first mines.

Now John's skills as a Merchant Navy officer were really needed. The mines were delivered on moving trolleys and these were placed on the railway lines below. Once in place wires, bottle-screws and shackles were produced and this dangerous cargo secured. All part of the skills of a man used to loading every kind of unusual cargo for transit around the world. Being present at the installation of the mine deck in Glasgow, John had insisted that extra eyebolts be fitted to the ship's side and deck plating. These additions were now to show their value. Dockers and the crew loaded three hundred and thirty old mines from the First World War. This was a record number, as subsequent mines were bigger and the ship could only load two hundred and sixty of the larger variety.

When loaded, the ship moved out into the River Humber for the crew to lash and secure the very dangerous cargo. Then, accompanied by two mine-sweepers, it proceeded northwards along the east coast to lay the first of the mines, which were to play a vital part in the countries defence against invasion. During this first operation the two mine-sweepers checked the depth of the mines to see if they were correctly laid. This proved a hazardous job as many of the mines proved unstable, possibly due to their age, and exploded soon after entering the water. Indeed

64

the crew was made well aware of the danger of the work they were carrying out as the ship pitched and shuddered from the explosions close to the stern. Following this mission in daylight the ship returned to Immingham and never again had an escort of mine-sweepers to lay mines in the North Sea.

Now the *Teviotbank* began the mammoth and dangerous task of laying 11,000 mines over the next eighteen months. Of course many incidents occurred during this time, but the luck of the ship was unbelievable. At first, in 1940, two destroyers would escort the ship to her destination – an anchorage in the Cromarty Firth. Later, as war-time demands grew on these ships, a sloop would suffice, and by the end of the year that vessel would have to escort a coastal convoy as well.

From the Firth the ship would then proceed to her current mining area. Usually at about 0430 in the morning the crew would go to mine-laying stations. John was in charge of the mining deck. Hands would unshackle the mines and propel them towards the stern doors, which were now open to the sea. At the door and on the end of the rail the mine would be held in check awaiting a signal by light and voice from the bridge to proceed. Then the brake would be released and the deadly mine with its carriage now acting as a sinker, would drop out into the sea. After a spectacular splash the mine would surface, showing its ugly horns, and then slowly sink out of sight. This operation would be repeated until the total cargo of two hundred and sixty mines had been laid. It was carried out with the utmost skill, often during darkness and in all kinds of weather, at a rate of one mine every nine seconds. After completion the ship would return to Immingham to load another cargo.

This routine was interrupted in April 1940 when the ship was ordered to Scapa Flow. There she joined the bulk of the home fleet, including HMS *Ramillies,* to await orders. She then sailed in the company of four destroyers, *Islex, Imogen, Ingelfield* and *Isis,* still not knowing her destination.

It did not help the morale of the crew when the band of the Royal Marines on *Ramillies* played *Wish Me Luck as You Wave Me Goodbye* as the convoy passed by. Then the White Ensign was substituted by the Red Ensign, causing even more concern.

In actual fact the ship was under orders to proceed to Norway to lay mines in Norwegian waters. This was tricky as Norway was not in the war at that time, and the ship was under orders not to fire at any Norwegian ship they encountered. However, the weather took a hand, and in a south-westerly gale the ship was unable to lay the mines. She waited off Stadlandet for a day, during which time the very violent seas smashed one of the lifeboats. Then a signal from the leading destroyer instructed *Teviotbank* to proceed at full speed to Sullom Voe, Shetland Islands, as the German invasion of Narvik was under way and German units were only sixty miles distant. The escort promptly disappeared in the direction of the enemy while the mine-layer departed westwards at top speed.

Back in the Shetland Islands the *Teviotbank* was to spend three weeks swinging at anchor before proceeding south once more to resume laying mines in the North Sea.

During the following months of 1940 two incidents in the North Sea show just how lucky the *Teviotbank* was in this period. On one run a torpedo from a German aircraft passed fifty feet astern of the ship. Later that same night another aircraft attacked the ship from the direction of her port quarter. As it happened the crew were at action stations but did not see the aircraft until the very last minute. Then a bomb exploded right under the stern, lifting the vessel several feet as it did so. At once the ship began to circle as her steering gear and the gyro-compass failed and all the lights went out. The crew was ordered to go to their stations for abandoning ship, however the engines did not fail and the vessel continued to circle in the middle of the convoy causing the other vessels to take evasive action. After some time, damage control parties reported that the ship was not leaking and the engine had been stopped in a normal manner. On the upper deck John organised parties to get a lifeboat compass and bring the emergency steering position on the stern into action. Lanterns were also obtained from the lifeboats, and painfully slowly *Teviotbank* was able to get under way and return to the Humber for repairs.

Indeed the damage to the systems had been severe, but three weeks later the ship was back at sea. On another occasion the ship had been under constant observation by E-boats. After the mines had been laid they would sail in and sweep the mines and sometimes lay mines of their own. The naval authorities therefore decreed that the *Teviotbank* and HMS *Plover,* another mine-layer, should be accompanied by two destroyers who would attack the E-boats on sight. On their way north they escorted a convoy and ran into a German mine-field laid by the same E-boats. The leading destroyer was so severely damaged that she had to be abandoned. Meanwhile the second destroyer had her bow blown off and only by the heroic efforts of her crew did she manage to reach port, stern first! Fortunately the *Teviotbank,* next in line, was able to stop, turn short round and get out of the mine-field without harm. She then, with *Plover,* had to escort the convoy back to the Humber, where on arrival they found the E-boats had swooped in behind them and mined the entrance.

There followed an anxious two days while, together with other shipping, they waited at anchor to enter the river whilst mine-sweepers swept the mines. On completion of this operation as senior naval ship present, the *Teviotbank* was due to be first to pass through the boomed entrance. But a large admiralty tug was waiting to dry dock at Hull, and as the mine-layer commenced to heave up her anchor, the tug sent a message by signal lamp. It read, 'Permission to proceed first as I need to catch the tide at Hull to enter dry dock.'

Commander King Harman replied, 'Permission granted. Proceed.'

As the tug passed through the entrance a mine that had been missed by the mine-sweepers exploded under her and she sank right in the channel. So the lucky ship had to wait again while the wreck was cleared before once more entering Immingham.

By this time Captain King Harman had come to regard John as his good luck charm, and although all the other Merchant Navy deck officers had left he would not allow John to be transferred.

During these months John would stay in a small pub on the Cleethorpes promenade. Here he would enjoy the company of the publican Chris and his wife Evelyn and the local seafaring community. On one occasion though, he became ill with shingles and after a visit from the doctor was told to stay in bed and not go to sea with the ship.

"I'm not having that. He is coming back whether he likes it or not," stormed the naval commander. He then sent four military policemen with a stretcher and they carried John back on board.

"I don't care if you can't work," he said to John, "I am not leaving my good luck behind in Cleethorpes."

By Christmas 1940 the *Teviotbank* was having a refit in Hull and most of the crew enjoyed a well-earned five day leave. Then the ship proceeded to the west coast of Scotland and worked for a while from the Kyle of Lochalsh and even ventured to the Faroe Islands on one occasion.

While at Lochalsh the mines were loaded from barges using the ship's derricks. Naturally, with mines swinging through the air, great care had to be taken during this operation. Here again John's experience as a Merchant Navy officer came into its own and the cargoes of mines were loaded without incident. However, for the most part, during the first six months of 1941 the *Teviotbank* operated out of Immingham.

9

Off to Fight the Japanese

In late May 1941, the ship laid the last of her mines in the North Sea and proceeded, in what seemed to be a routine way, to the Kyle of Lochalsh. Then, almost casually, a message was received from the admiralty to proceed to Falmouth. Something was afoot, the ship's mine-laying days in home waters were over.

It seems almost incredible now, but since she had been commissioned HMS *Teviotbank* had already laid 14,000 mines and a great barrier existed all the way from the North of Scotland to the English Channel.

In St. Ives, in the early days of June 1941, Eric was not quite four years old. At this tender age the war meant very little. The family lived in an old Victorian terraced house in Bellair Terrace. Downstairs the house was lit by gas and they used candles upstairs.

Now, on an early day of June, just before dawn, Eric was peacefully asleep when there was a rattle on the bedroom window; someone was throwing small pebbles at the panes. Moving across the room he could see his uncle William standing in the small front garden. Uncle Will, as he was known, was an important member in the immediate family – he was the owner of a telephone! It had not been possible for John to let his family know he was coming to Falmouth, but Uncle Will brought the news and immediately preparations began for the journey to the

69

port by train.

Later that day, John settled his family in a seaside guest-house close to the docks. Then next morning, as a very small, excited four year old, Eric climbed the gangway from the eastern arm in Falmouth Docks to board HMS *Teviotbank*. The sailor at the gangway saluted his father, while Chief Engineer Mr Sinclair shouted a greeting from the boat deck as they entered the ship's accommodation.

While at Falmouth two new multiple 0.5mm guns, together with two single Oerlikons, were installed. Some changes were made to the accommodation and extra crew joined. After another overhaul of the engines and the provision of extra stores and fine weather awnings it was obvious that the ship was bound for warmer waters.

Certainly as the ship prepared to sail, Great Britain was having a very tough time indeed. It had been a year since the army had been evacuated from Dunkirk and all the main cities and ports in Britain were under attack. Over 20,000 Londoners had been killed in air-raids on the capital. But the *Teviotbank* remained a lucky ship and Falmouth was not attacked during her visit. This break was to be the last leave John was to have before the ship decommissioned in August 1944, three years later.

Now a senior officer in the executive branch, John sailed with the ship to Liverpool and there the *Teviotbank* joined a convoy to Freetown in West Africa. This voyage took eighteen days and they escaped attack from the numerous U-boats hunting them. Fourteen days later they arrived in Capetown. There the ship remained for a week with the crew experiencing wonderful treatment by the South African people ashore. Then on to Durban for a couple of days and fresh bunker coal.

Now escorted by HMS *Dragon*, the ship sailed by way of Mauritius, The Maldive Islands and Ceylon, to Singapore, the ship's final destination. Here the preparations were going ahead to defend the colony from the sea. After a refit and boiler clean the *Teviotbank* began laying mines in the approaches to the port.

During this period the battleships *Prince of Wales* and *Repulse* had sailed from Singapore following the attack by the Japanese on Pearl Harbour. As the mines were being laid the chilling news came that the Japanese had sunk the two mighty warships. Christmas was somewhat subdued as the *Teviotbank* awaited orders in the roads.

Just before the New Year, John was ashore when an air-raid occurred and orders were given for all service staff to return to their places of duty. Amid the confusion of the bombs and fires he ran down to the waterside and grabbed an empty sampan and paddled it out to the anchorage. There he was able to jump on to the partly lowered gangway as the ship was actually heaving in the anchor chain prior to sailing. Once again the tremendous luck of the *Teviotbank* was to allow her to escape the clutches of the enemy.

Captain King Harman had been a Singapore pilot for many years and he was aware of many other ways out of the islands than proceeding down the main channel. Ahead of the mine-layer a merchantman ran straight into an ambush. Seeing the flames and hearing the gunfire, the *Teviotbank* turned into the smaller channels and emerged unscathed and undetected by the Japanese. Quickly and with some courage she laid her full cargo of mines and fled to Batavia in Java.

From Batavia she was due to join a convoy to Australia. However, engine trouble developed and the *Teviotbank* remained behind. Again the luck held as the convoy suffered very heavy casualties.

Later, sailing independently, *Teviotbank* proceeded to Trincomalee in Ceylon. Here she was to stay and lay a number of mines, mainly in the Andaman Islands, during the coming months. In April once again good luck saved her from a horrendous attack by the Japanese. It was known that the Japanese fleet was close and all ships at Trincomalee were ordered to raise steam and proceed to sea as an air attack was expected on the port.

Ahead of the convoy was a battle fleet led by the aircraft carrier HMS *Hermes* and some smaller units. On the 8th of April 1942 a very large concentration of Japanese fighter bombers flew past the convoy and attacked the aircraft carrier and her escorts.

It was a prolonged battle and the carrier was sunk. The Japanese aim to attack warships led them to ignore the mine-layer, fully loaded, steaming in the middle of the convoy. While on their way back from the attack the planes did drop a few bombs on the fringe of the convoy, well away from the ship.

One unfortunate vessel, the SS *Sagaing,* was unable to sail and was bombed at her anchorage. On their return to port the convoy found the vessel burning and abandoned in the roadstead. Following this attack the *Teviotbank* was to move her base to Bombay in western India.

Here she was to stay until 1944. She did spend some time in Aden laying mines but for most of the time she lay at anchor outside the Indian port.

At this time John sent a large number of letters to his son Eric. At the top of each one would be a drawing of a ship, plane, lighthouse and many other scenes, which helped to illustrate his narrative.

John was promoted to Lieutenant Commander early in 1942 and as such he became the senior executive officer on board. During this time at Bombay most of the crew were relieved, but John and Archie Sinclair, the original chief engineer, remained, and in fact served out the time that the *Teviotbank* remained in Naval Service.

In March 1944 the ship sailed northwards through the Suez Canal and passed the units of the surrendered Italian Fleet. In the Mediterranean she now took part in the Italian campaign, laying mines and being present at Torre Annunziata and Naples.

She came under attack from Junkers 88s on a number of occasions and her guns fought back with some effect. It was reported that two aircraft were damaged attacking the mine-layer while, of course, her luck continued to hold as she was not hit in these actions. So in early June HMS *Teviotbank* laid her last mine-field without opposition off the Isle of Capri.

In four and a half years this plucky converted merchantman had laid over 20,000 mines and had become a major Naval unit. Like so much of his sea service John had served through it all with little praise.

Action stations on HMS *Teviotbank* in 1941.

Commander King Harman, the captain of
HMS *Teviotbank* in 1941.

SS *Sagaing* at Trincomalee in 1943, bombed by Japanese.

Lieutenant Commander John Kemp RNR,
second in command HMS *Teviotbank*, 1944.

HMS *Buchanness* leaving Vancouver.

SS *Rowanbank*, previously *Samford*.
Captain John Kemp's first command.

Loading manganese ore by hand (and head),
SS *Rowanbank*, Calcutta.

Captain and officers of the SS *Rowanbank*, 1949

Incredible fire and heavy weather damage to a cargo
of tractors and bulk sulphur aboard the SS *Rowanbank*.

John Kemp captain's MV *Meadowbank*
under Sydney Bridge, Australia in 1953.

Ship's cat Mary Meadowbank, 1952.

MV *Fleetbank* at Bombay, India, 1954.

MV *Fleetbank*
passes through the
English Narrows in
the Magellan Straits,
Chile, 1954.

MV *Fleetbank* off
Accra in Ghana,
discharging bales of
sacking from India
into surf canoes.

Tristan da Cunha
in the South
Atlantic as the
MV *Fleetbank*
passes by.

MV *City of Johannesburg* with apprentice Eric Kemp on board, pictured from the MV *Glenbank*, off South Africa, on which Captain John Kemp was in command.

MV *Glenbank* loading phosphate at Nauru in the South Pacific.

"I prevented your transfer to other ships on promotion because of my belief in you being my good luck," was the comment of Commander King Harman as he left the ship in 1944. "Also, I have not recommended you for a medal, as the naval officers need them for their future appointments after the war. I am very sorry and you would be well within your rights to think that I have treated you badly."

John accepted these apologies without complaint; remarking in later life, "I was glad to come through it alive, even if it had cost me a lot of money."

So, after a slow trip home, the *Teviotbank* returned to the port where it all began, Greenock, on the Clyde.

Many crew-members were to leave the vessel there but John was to have one more notable event. Due to illness the captain left at Greenock, and for her last trip under the White Ensign John commanded the ship on her passage to the River Tyne and decommissioning.

It is interesting to note that the *Teviotbank* went on to give sterling service as a tramp steamer until 1971, a real tribute to the British shipbuilders John Readhead and Sons.

At this point John was of the opinion that the Admiralty would release him and he would be able to return to the Bank Line. But the Lords of the Admiralty had a high regard for John and he was not released at this point. He went on to serve as second in command of HMS *Athene* and HMS *Buchanness,* both seaplane carriers, and was not released before the end of the war. The *Buchanness* was, in fact, a working repair ship, and was about to sail from Vancouver fully stored for the Japanese invasion when the war came to an end.

Now the war was over, John had a really good leave at home, and by the end of 1945 he was ready once more to resume his Merchant Navy career.

At the beginning of 1946 John was once again at sea as chief officer of the twin-screw motor vessel *Irisbank,* of 5,626 gross tonnage. This vessel had been built at the yard of Workman Clark, Belfast in 1930 and was a standard Bank Line motor ship. At that time she was sailing on the round the world service calling at

American gulf ports, Australia, New Zealand and the Pacific Islands, thence back to the UK via the Suez Canal.

During the year he spent on this ship there was a very pleasant two months in Belfast having a really comprehensive refit. Ann and Eric spent the summer school holiday on the ship. Many friends were made in the peaceful city at that time, with visits in their company to the beautiful Northern Ireland countryside. These journeys included the Mourne Mountains and the Giants Causeway and were a real treat for a family separated for much of the war.

The return trip to the ship would usually entail a ride in one of the famous Belfast trams. On more than one occasion the friendly drivers would let Eric, at the tender age of nine, drive the tram before its last stop at the dock gates. Captain Allen was in command at this time and he ran a very happy ship and allowed John's family to really enjoy themselves during the stay.

All too soon though, this period was over and the ship was in the port of New York loading for New Zealand. When the Marine Superintendent Captain Andoe boarded, he brought good news for John.

"You are to proceed to Vancouver via Montreal by train and there join the SS *Samford* which we currently manage. You will command the vessel on her voyage back to Belfast with a timber cargo. Congratulations Captain!"

Those words were the ones for which John had waited many years, and he started packing his gear with a will.

On the 30th of January 1947, Captain John Kemp started his three-day journey to the west coast of Canada to join his first command in the merchant service. On his arrival in Vancouver a young man walked up to him as he left the crowded train.

"Captain Kemp, I presume," he said, as he offered to help John with his luggage.

"How did you know me?" said the startled John.

"My advice, sir," he replied, "was that any British ship master could be easily recognised by the fact that he would be wearing a navy blue mackintosh, a trilby with a short brim and carrying a small mahogany box containing a sextant. So, sir, as you see, it is totally correct and I had no trouble in finding you in the crowd."

As it happened, the SS *Samford* was loading timber and grain at a place called Chemainus on Vancouver Island. This entailed a four-hour journey by steamer to Nanaimo. There, in bitter cold and driving snow, John had to bargain with a taxi driver to get him to a customs post and release his gear, which was under seal, then drive thirty miles over icy roads to the timber wharf at Chemainus. His expenses claimed for this journey were fifty-seven dollars.

At midnight, in falling snow, he saw his first command, still in battle grey paint and loading a massive deck cargo of timber. Over the next few days John had to visit the master, Captain Sinclair, who was lying in Hospital with a broken thigh, and take over the paper work of the ship. It was also necessary to visit Vancouver on ship's business and become acquainted with the ship and the crew.

SS *Samford* was a liberty vessel built at Joshua Hendy Iron Works, Sunnyvale, California, for the United States War Shipping Administration in 1943. At that time she was chartered to the Ministry of War transport and managed by the Bank Line. She had a gross tonnage of 7,262 tons and was powered by a three cylinder steam reciprocating engine giving a speed of ten knots and capable of carrying a cargo of 10,200 tons. These vessels were built with an all welded construction and many broke in half in the years after the war. This almost happened to the *Samford* but that comes later on in the story.

The vessel set sail for Belfast carrying a full cargo, with over a thousand tons of timber on deck. The homeward passage was to take forty-two days, passing through the Panama Canal. In the Atlantic the winter weather was to take its toll and soaked the deck cargo with seawater; while the use of fuel and fresh water, stored low down in the ship, caused the ship's stability to reduce considerably. Indeed, by the time the vessel entered Belfast Loch she had listed to starboard with a frightening slant. So the crew was very relieved to finish the voyage safely.

Although John had only been in command for fifty days he now faced the task of completing all the ship's bills, wages and other accounts relating to a crew of fifty-seven over the two years since the vessel had left the United Kingdom. Then all the paper work had to be changed as the vessel was bought by the Bank Line and renamed SS *Rowanbank*. The cargo had to be discharged and a new crew signed on; not to mention Customs, Immigration, Food and the Board of Trade Inspectors, all needing time to talk to the master of the ship.

John was already showing he was born for the job. All went without a hitch, and as with the rest of his life few people appreciated just how hard he worked to accomplish this smoothly.

As the *Rowanbank* discharged, orders were received to proceed to the Gabon River in West Africa, there to load a cargo for the United Africa Company (later called the Palm Line).

10

A Troublesome Ship

This was the last ministry cargo for the *Rowanbank,* and at once John showed his worth and professional confidence.

Another ex-liberty vessel had also been chartered to collect West African cargo. She was owned and run by the Blue Funnel Line, Alfred Holts of Liverpool, and had loaded 3,000 tons of earth ballast at Liverpool over the week prior to the *Rowanbank* sailing. Now both vessels headed out into the Irish Sea together. The *Rowanbank* had caught up a week by not loading any solid ballast at all.

A severe south-easterly storm struck on that first day in April. At Milford Haven an American liberty vessel was wrecked and the Blue Funnel vessel sought shelter off North Wales. Not so the *Rowanbank.* John filled the space on either side of the ship's propeller shaft with seawater, so getting the propeller deeper into the water. This did, of course, have to be done with care, for if the vessel got beam on to the storm the water in the hold could cause a dramatic effect on the rolling of the ship and even cause her to capsize. Fortunately the *Rowanbank* rode out the storm and proceeded south ahead of the second vessel on charter.

On arrival in West African waters the crew cleaned out the now empty hold and the ship was immediately ready to load. Realising that the *Rowanbank* was ahead of the Blue Funnel ship, the agents Elder Dempster lines then switched cargoes of the two ships, with the Bank Line vessel loading the more important cargo in Lagos, Nigeria and Takoradi on the Gold Coast (Sekondi-Takoradi in Ghana today).

The *Rowanbank* then loaded the heaviest cargo of timber and bagged cargo ever shipped from West Africa in a liberty vessel. She returned to Liverpool on the 16th June 1947, just two months and sixteen days after leaving Belfast. Indeed, it was probably the shortest foreign going voyage of a Bank Line vessel up to that time.

Then, as a very special favour, the captain and the chief engineer were allowed to bring their families for the short coastal voyage around the north of Scotland to Middlesbrough. During the voyage John's son Eric was allowed to steer the vessel and announced with conviction, "I want to be a captain like my dad."

One inducement at the time was the excellent food on the ship. Eric would never forget the taste of fried egg and bacon twice a week and the chicken dinner on Sundays. After the shortages of food at home that was indeed real heaven.

John and the crew were to pay for that short trip, as the next two voyages of the ship were twenty months and seven days, and twenty-two months and two days respectively, with only a four day leave between them.

Over those four years the ship was to circle the globe on a number of occasions. Ports in Egypt, Arabia, India, Burma, Australia, New Zealand, USA, Japan and Argentina were all visited and cargoes loaded and discharged. The *Rowanbank* was a difficult command, however, and two incidents in those years clearly show the troubles and trials of a tramp master serving in a liberty vessel.

In October 1949, the ship loaded a full cargo of flour in Adelaide destined for India. On the 10th of the month the *Rowanbank* was in a position some 600 miles from the port and pitching and rolling violently in a westerly gale. She was shipping heavy seas along her full length and making a speed of only two knots. At about seven o'clock in the evening a very big sea broke over the bow and rolled over the hatches and against the midship's accommodation. As the vessel shuddered and vibrated and rose on the next wave a loud metallic crack was heard throughout the ship.

John was on the bridge at this time and considered it was too dangerous to send anyone on to the deck to find out what had happened. As the vessel was now acting in a very sluggish manner and having steering difficulties, something had to be done at once.

"Warn the crew we are going to turn around stern to the sea," he ordered the third officer. "She will probably roll heavily and could break in half. Have your life-jackets ready and be ready to abandon ship if it goes wrong."

With great skill John allowed the bow to blow off the wind and using the engine at the right moment managed to turn the ship stern to the sea. Then putting the engine at slow speed astern he managed to stabilise the situation and the long wait for daylight began.

At daybreak the weather had eased a little and the men on the bridge could see that the bow was moving independently of the stern at times. Out on the fore deck, just forward of the accommodation, a crack had developed right across the deck and five feet down either side, and with the movement of the ship it was slowly lengthening. Seawater had entered number three hold but the presence of the tightly packed bags of flour was holding the ship together.

Action was needed to keep the ship in one piece. At first a wire rope was threaded around the ship's accommodation and the mast house between number two and three holds. Then with the steam-driven main deck winch the wire was tightened to ease the strain on the crack. Three engineers drilled holes on either side of the crack and bolted pieces of steel across it. Whilst doing this they were often up to their waists in water and were forced to hang on to life-lines rigged for the purpose.

Now in moderating weather, the ship began slowly to steam towards Adelaide. This passage was to take three days and throughout this time watch had to be kept that the weather did not deteriorate again. While entering the St. Vincent Gulf the ship could have made for a safe anchorage or a smaller port. This had to be considered with the safety of all on board in mind. However, if the ship reached Adelaide, repair facilities were on hand and the owners and insurers would be saved a great deal of time and expense. After assessing the situation and listening to some conflicting advice John proceeded on to the larger port.

On arrival the crack was found to have travelled fourteen feet down one side of the ship and five feet on the other. Surveyors boarded at this point and the *Rowanbank* had a prolonged stay in the port to discharge her cargo and effect repairs. Before moving into the docks the vessel had to anchor for a period of forty-eight hours while micrometer measurements were made to see if the crack was still increasing.

The safe return of the *Rowanbank* was indeed a tribute to the captain, officers and crew who had worked in such treacherous conditions to bring the vessel back to port. It was to take over two months to complete repairs and the ship resumed her voyage to India on the 23rd of December 1949, just in time to celebrate Christmas at sea; hardly a novelty for a British tramp skipper in those days.

While in Adelaide, John was to have an interesting meeting with some old friends. During the two-month period he was in the habit of walking from the dock area to the city and back for exercise. On one such walk in December he noticed that a thunderstorm was heading towards him. As he walked past some traffic lights, an empty taxi pulled up for the red signal. Seeing the threat from the thunder and lightning, John opened the door and asked to be taken to the docks.

The driver, who was sitting with his back to him as he proceeded, remarked that John had a Cornish accent.

"Where do you come from?" John asked.

"St. Ives," said the voice inside the darkened cab.

"Stop," said John. "So do I."

As the driver turned on the light, John could see that it was a childhood friend called John Phillips. As children they had been members of the Doble's Wall Gang in the town. This group, some eight strong, had used the old wall in front of the Kemp barber's shop as their meeting place. It still stands today in front of Hart's

80

Ice Cream Parlour.

As they talked, memories of the busy harbour and the narrow streets of St. Ives came flooding back. And it turned out that three more members of the gang lived close to the city: John Phillip's two brothers and Jim Ward. Also in the port at that time was Captain Leslie Mitchell, another gang member and still serving in the Hain Line. So they all had a great reunion and sang mostly Cornish carols for the coming of the festive season.

Another friend who visited John frequently on his many visits to Adelaide over the years was the famous cricketer Donald Bradman. He was involved in ship insurance and frequently bought tickets to see international rugby matches and other large events held while the ship was in port in Australia. John would often dine with his famous guest but commented in later years that the subject of cricket did not feature very much in their conversations. (This was much to his son's annoyance as he is a great cricket fan, unlike his dad.)

In early June 1950 the *Rowanbank* loaded a general cargo in the Gulf of Mexico for Wellington, New Plymouth and Auckland in New Zealand. Most of her general cargo was for Wellington and this included a large number of tractors. In the lower holds the cargo consisted of bulk sulphur for Auckland and New Plymouth. On the 17th of July the ship was approaching Wellington, near Cape Palliser in the Cook Strait. A severe westerly storm was in progress with a big westerly swell. The ship was rolling very heavily and consideration was being given to heaving to and waiting for some ease in the weather. At about nine o'clock in the evening, John was called to the bridge to hear loud banging sounds coming from number two hold and he immediately ordered the ship to turn into the wind and heave to.

While they were waiting, thick smoke could be seen coming from the ventilators of the hold. John ordered the chief officer to lead a party of officers and crew to close the ventilators and check all openings around the hatch and see they were sealed. Then the holds were filled with steam from the ship's fire fighting equipment in order to control the fire.

After two hours of fighting the fire and stabilising the

situation, *Rowanbank* again set her course for Wellington, eventually entering the port during the next morning to be boarded by the local fire brigade.

When the hatch was opened flames leapt into the air, needing immediate work by the waiting firemen, then an amazing sight was revealed. As a result of the stormy weather the welded bolts attached to the ship's side had broken free, releasing the tractors. With the heat of the fire below (possibly caused by sparks as the tractors moved) the 'tween-deck hatch boards and beams had collapsed onto the sulphur. The ladders into the hold were glowing red and the fire brigade had a great deal of work to do before anyone could get below. Seventeen tractors had emerged from their packing cases and were extensively damaged in the lower hold. The prompt action of heaving the ship to and closing down the ventilation had saved the vessel.

Following repairs the ship discharged the rest of her cargo and prepared to load copra in the Pacific Islands for London. At last John's four-year service with the old liberty vessel was coming to an end.

Missing Christmas as usual, John docked the *Rowanbank* in London on the 27th of December 1950 and paid the crew off next day.

While berthed at Tilbury both his wife and son joined him, as they had four years before. As his last duty in the ship John brought the vessel to South Shields for a refit over the New Year period.

During this short voyage Eric made his life a misery pleading to go on watch during the passage. Eventually it was agreed that he should keep a watch with Mr Wigan, the chief officer, from four to eight in the morning. However, at only thirteen years of age, Eric was not convinced that he would be called for the watch. Indeed he had to be led back to his cabin at two and three in the morning after asking the second officer if it was yet time to go up on the bridge. But in the end there was the thrill of marking the position of the ship as she passed the channel buoys at the entrance to the Humber.

"I really do want to go to sea, Dad," Eric announced to his

father as they sailed up the coast next morning.

"It's a lonely old life Eric," he said. "If you really want to I won't stop you. Next year I will see if you can be trained on the HMS *Worcester* at Greenhithe in Kent, if you are still of the same mind. That's a rather better start to a sea-going life than I had on the *Trevessa*."

One incident occurred on this short passage which showed John's harder side. It seemed the third officer had a really good celebration over the New Year, and having been overseas for two years one could easily understand the temptation. He had then been required to be in charge of the bridge watch on the night of the second of January. As the ship passed Great Yarmouth John had found the tired mate sleeping on the bridge wing dodger.

After seeing that the ship was in a safe position, John filled a bucket with ice cold water and poured it all over the sleeping officer. As he awoke with a start he had to face a furious master.

"How dare you risk the safety of this ship and her crew? If I ever find you taking your duties so lightly in future, I will make sure you never sail in a Bank Line vessel again," said John in a voice like thunder.

A shivering officer could only splutter his apologies, but he had learned a very necessary lesson.

Soon the ship was in the hands of the shipyard and John's family went ashore to take a cab to the station to catch a train. It was significant that John did not look back as he left. It had been a long hard tour of service and now he came home for his first long leave in four years. It is noteworthy that the officers and engineers of the *Rowanbank* presented John with a silver salver as a mark of their high regard for his skill and seamanship during this voyage.

Much later the ship was to run aground off Bombay, under a different captain, of course. Then the Bank Line sold the ship in 1959 to Hong Kong owners who renamed her *Taiwind*. She was then in collision with a Panamanian tanker called *St. Matthew* in the Indian Ocean in 1966, as a result of which she became a total constructive loss.

In April 1951 John joined the MV *Meadowbank*, 7,307 gross

tons, as master. This vessel was built at W. Doxford and Sons, and completed in 1945. The three-cylinder Doxford engine gave a speed of eleven knots, but in head winds this quickly reduced due to the lack of power in the engine. Much of the design had come from the government vessels of the war. With improved accommodation, electric winches and capstans it was better than the average tramp of the day.

John was to spend two and a half years on the ship with Ann joining him for seventeen months of the voyage, in Bremen. For the crew just the heartbreaking sight of the white cliffs of Dover, as the ship delivered a cargo of copra and sailed for the USA without calling at a British port.

Ann had a particular friend on this ship – a black and white female cat that she named 'Mary Meadowbank'. This followed a St. Ives tradition of calling their cats by two names. This cat had a nasty habit of disappearing just before the ship sailed to see if she could find a boyfriend. Ann would become most concerned, especially as John would be quite happy to lose the cat. On board the cat only caused him problems with the various port authorities.

"I'll give you some remuneration if you can find the cat," she would whisper to the apprentices just before sailing time. "But don't tell the captain, will you?" From what can be gathered the apprentices had a nice little earner on that voyage.

Eric was at that time a boarder at Truro School, and his mother had to leave the vessel at Accra on the Ivory Coast in order to help him get a place on the training ship HMS *Worcester,* before he could go to sea as an apprentice.

This disembarkation entailed being lifted in a wooden box (called a Mammy Chair) by the ship's derricks and being lowered on to a surfboat. Then followed a dangerous trip through the surf to a sloping beach, before a taxi ride to the airport. Today the modern port of Tema has replaced the port of Accra and the surfboats are only a memory.

On the 12th of October 1953 the *Meadowbank* docked in Avonmouth after a voyage of twenty-nine months, during which time King George VI had died and Queen Elizabeth II had been crowned. In all the ship had steamed over 100,000 miles and visited the USA, South Africa, Nigeria, Germany, Australia, New Zealand, India, Ceylon and Pakistan.

In Greenhithe, Kent, Cadet (Eric) Kemp had been summoned to see Commander Steels VC, the captain of the *Worcester*.

"It seems your father has had a very long voyage, young Kemp," he said. "I have just read his letter and am granting you a three day special leave to go to Avonmouth."

It was to be a magic time for Eric. Firstly the ship was discharging her cargo and he was able to observe the officers at close hand. Then for the only time in his life he was able to see a professional football match in the company of his father. It was a game between Bristol City and Ipswich in the old third division of the football league. In the evening there was a visit to the Bristol theatre to see the popular musical *Oklahoma*. But all too soon it was back to his studies while his father and mother returned home to St. Ives.

It is interesting to note that the voyage of the *Meadowbank* had passed without any real comment from the Bank Line management. Their representatives checked all the accounts, cargo bills and reports of incidents (all minor) without any real questions.

That was the real skill of a good tramp master. John himself said on one occasion: "I always knew the cheapest way out of any problem that the ship might have. I have only ever had one disagreement with the company and that was over catering bills being too expensive." It seemed that he well understood the truth of the saying that a well-fed ship was an efficient one. He stood his ground against these complaints and was never questioned again on that subject in his sea-going career.

11

New Ships and Old

It seems remarkable now, but up to this time John had never been in a ship with either radar equipment or a gyrocompass. His navigating skills were based on a magnetic compass, an accurate chronometer, a good sounding machine, a radio direction finder, up-to-date charts and a sextant. All this was to change, as he was about to get his first experience of the new tonnage now being built by the Bank Line.

In February 1954 he was asked to fly from London to Buenos Aires to join MV *Fleetbank*. Captain Palmer, her master, had been hospitalised and the vessel needed a replacement quickly. This meant hurriedly packing his seagoing gear and travelling to London Airport post-haste. There, on a Sunday morning at 9.15am, John was a passenger in a BOAC Argonaut airliner on a thirty-nine hour flying time journey to Buenos Aires. The plane stopped at Madrid, Lisbon, Dakar, Recife, Rio and Montevideo before arriving at its destination. At the airport the company agent collected him in his car to take him to the ship.

"Come on Captain, your ship is due to sail, we must get a move on," he announced with gusto. That smile soon waned as the car suffered a blow-out and he had to ask the weary captain to help change the wheel. This meant that after a prolonged journey on congested roads, John had to take over the ship and prepare for sailing within a couple of hours of arrival.

MV *Fleetbank* had sailed as a new ship from the Belfast shipyard of Harland and Wolff on the 14th October 1953. She was a steel motor ship of 5,690 gross tons. Her six-cylinder engine gave a service speed of 14.5 knots and she had a length of 449 feet 6 inches with a beam of 59 feet 4 inches, fully loaded she had a draft of 26 feet.

She was equipped with radar but no gyrocompass. Her spacious cabins and light and airy saloon were a complete contrast to the older ships in which John had previously sailed. He was to remain with this ship for nineteen months, mainly trading between India, South Africa and South America. These voyages entailed passing through the Straits of Magellan and calling at many small ports in Chile and Peru.

While on passage across the South Atlantic the ship would pass within six miles of the lonely island of Tristan da Cunha. During the winter month of July 1954 an albatross landed on the deck and stayed for a twenty-four hour period while the ship was in this area.

In January 1955, for example, the ship called at fifteen ports from Punta Arenas, near Cape Horn, to Paita in the north of Peru. In many cases these were places where the ship anchored off the coast and barges came alongside to take the cargo, which consisted mostly of gunny and other jute from India.

On arrival a whole batch of officials would board from customs, immigration, harbour-masters and even military representatives. All would need entertaining, or a bribe, for the ship to pass on her way without problems. On most occasions, in the smaller ports, the formalities would take longer than the actual discharge of cargo. All of this, together with the short passage time between ports, meant a gruelling time for the ship's captain.

Eventually the ship loaded sugar at Buenos Aires for Port Sudan. At that port a new crew joined the ship and John and his crew returned to Southend in a chartered aircraft in September 1955.

By the New Year of 1956 there were two seafarers in the family. In December 1955 John had the very considerable satisfaction of helping Eric sign indentures as an apprentice in the Ellerman and Bucknall Steamship Company of London.

In actual fact both of them visited Mr Cogar at his home in St. Ives. Now long retired from his position with the Hain Steamship Company he still had an active mind and many memories of his office days. After signing Eric's indentures as a witness, as he had some thirty-five years before for John, he wished him well.

"I hope you do as well as your father, young man, he has been a real credit to St. Ives."

Shortly after, on New Year's Eve, Eric sailed out of Birkenhead bound for India on an ex-ministry vessel the SS *City of Cardiff*, 6,987 gross tons. Bound, as it turned out, for Calcutta, just as his father before him.

John then had a bit of a shock in April, as he was asked to join an older ship – the MV *Glenbank* in Rotterdam. Built in 1924 by Harland Wolff of Glasgow, she was one of six vessels still sailing for the Bank Line some 31 years later. These ships were the very first motor ships built for the company and they served with distinction until 1959.

John was allowed to take Ann with him once more and they travelled to the continent together to join the ship. MV *Glenbank* was a 5,151 gross ton vessel with a six-cylinder engine and her service speed was a stately 10 knots.

The ship was sailing for Trinidad the next day, so it was all hustle and bustle as John took over the ship, checked his accounts, papers, crew, stores and so on. As he also dealt with officials such as customs, port, health and agents, Ann quietly sat doing her knitting and only speaking when spoken to. She watched with interest as the pilot boarded and the old vessel was towed out of her berth into the river and then steamed down the river to the sea. Just before the pilot left at the Maas buoy, John briefly came down to the cabin to collect some letters for the post.

"I've got a ship that's thirty-one years old, with just a magnetic compass, a very old radio direction finder and no radar," he said, "and we are heading down into the Dover Straits with extensive fog banks all around."

Captain John Kemp is honoured to take command of this
brand new ship, the MV *Crestbank*, launched at Belfast, 1957.

MV *Crestbank* on builder's trials, Belfast.

MV *Streambank*. Another brand new vessel captained by John Kemp, anchored off New Plymouth, New Zealand in 1961.

Buckingham Palace, 1962. John Kemp, with his wife Ann Kemp and daughter-in-law Jill Kemp, after receiving his MBE from the Queen.

John Kemp taking noon sights somewhere in
the Indian Ocean, 1963.

MV *Inverbank* on maiden voyage at Durban, South Africa, 1963.

MV *Laganbank* on passage to Hamburg, Germany.

Launch of MV *Carronbank* at Belfast, 1957.
John Kemp centre with Lord Inverforth on right.

MV *Weybank* loading 54ft launch *Vonu* at the
West India Dock, London.

MV *Weybank* with *Vonu* loaded on deck.

John Kemp with his wife Ann on his retirement
in 1970, after fifty years at sea.

Mike Belsey (Trinity House) presents a certificate to
John Kemp on his retirement as a Commissioner of
Pilotage for St. Ives bay in 1986.

John Kemp in the Hain Room of the St. Ives Museum
with Ian Bell, son of Douglas Bell who
survived the sinking of the *Trevessa*.

On leave John Kemp liked nothing better than to take a
working passage on a St. Ives fishing boat. He travelled on this
boat, *Rose of Sharon,* in 1967.

"You have always coped before, in both war and peace, I'm sure you will again," Ann replied, giving a ready smile.

"Very funny!" he said as he left to go back to the bridge. But he did, and no one really noticed voyages like that one brought to a safe conclusion. It is only if you lose the ship or have a collision that anyone notices.

As it was, the old ship turned out to be one of the happiest ships John sailed in. Also on board sailing with her husband was the chief engineer's wife, a Mrs Wright. The two ladies got on well together and soon formed a card school with some of the ship's officers.

At one stage Ann set to in the ship's galley and taught the Indian cook how to make quite a good Cornish pasty. The voyage was to last twelve months and seventeen days. In that time the *Glenbank* visited Trinidad, New Zealand, Nauru, India, Argentina, Pakistan and Chile before returning to Rotterdam. During the passage between India and Argentina the ship was to pass the MV *City of Johannesburg*, 8,207 gross tons, a smart twelve passenger vessel on passage from Capetown to Port Elizabeth, on which Eric was serving. Due to the limited radio equipment on the *Glenbank* they could only exchange messages within 500 miles of one another and then only by Morse code.

It was on this voyage in 1956, while on the passage between New Zealand and Nauru, that John and Ann celebrated their twenty-fifth wedding anniversary, with John working – just as he had done on their honeymoon.

It was in the following year that John considered the highlight of his career came about. Ship masters in those days considered it to be a great honour and the fulfilment of their dreams to take a new ship away from the builders, and in April 1957 John was appointed the Master of the *Crestbank* then being built at the Harland & Wolff yard in Belfast.

While standing by at the builder's yard he was to join the directors at the launch of the *Carronbank*, the first ship of this new class. *Crestbank* was the second in the series of six ships built at the yard for the company. Her gross tonnage was 6,459 tons with a length of 483 feet, a beam of 63 feet and a draft of 26

j

feet. Service speed was 15 knots developed from her 6-cylinder diesel engine supplied by the builders. She was complete with all the modern aids to navigation including gyrocompass, radar and automatic helmsman, not to mention the latest radio equipment.

John was really on top of the world. *Crestbank* carried a crew of 16 Europeans and 49 Indians in spacious well lit and tastefully furnished cabins. While an owner's suite meant that the vessel could carry passengers from time to time.

However, the command of a new ship was always a tricky operation and great care had to be taken during the first months. Despite extensive trials, equipment was always likely to fail and the master was called upon to have his wits about him at all times. A typical example happened to the vessel as she approached the Goodwin Sands in the English Channel bound for Rotterdam.

Proceeding at 19 knots with the assistance of a tidal flow, the ship's engines and power failed. At once the ship's steering failed and the vessel was plunged into darkness. John, who was on the bridge, shouted, "Quickly, man, get forward and let go both anchors." This order was carried out with alacrity and the ship pulled up with less than a half mile to spare from the nearest sandbank. Also in these situations good engineers were vital and they had the ship under way in less than 20 minutes.

June 2nd 1958 found the *Crestbank* berthed in Colombo while substantial riots were occurring all over Ceylon between Sinhalese and Tamil citizens. The ship had been loading tea for South America. When work ceased on the evening of the 2nd of June, all was quiet in the port. A messenger arrived on board with a summons for the captain to attend a meeting at naval headquarters immediately. On arrival at the naval base John found the captains of five other ships already present with their various ship's agents. Four of these ships were British: *Clan Mackinnon*, *Mullah*, *Magdapur* and *City of Colchester*, while the other was the French ship *Laos*.

Taking the chair at this meeting was Commodore Royce de Mal OBE of the Royal Ceylon Navy. He outlined to the assembled meeting the very serious position the Government found itself in with regard to the rioting in the city. Living in camps in the vicinity of Colombo were over 5,000 refugees, and these Tamil people were under attack from the Sinhalese majority. That day the authorities had learned that there was major violence planned against these camps. Meanwhile in the north of the country similar attacks were being made on Sinhalese people.

It was proposed to requisition the six ships in Colombo to take the refugees to Kankesanturai in the north of the island. From there they would be taken by road to Jaffna. Meanwhile in the north a Japanese vessel, *Hizakawa Maru,* would be bringing Sinhalese refugees south to Colombo.

As all of these moves were confidential the ship's masters and agents were unable to contact the owners to inform them of their intentions. Not unnaturally the skippers began to disagree and demanded the chance to get their owners' permission. It very quickly became apparent that the naval officers were in deadly earnest and that no arguing was to be allowed. John, sensing the difficulties and delays that would occur if the deadlock were not broken, was the first to agree that his vessel could be used for the operation.

"I think," he said, "that it would be wise for us to agree to help the government with their problem. Unrest here will delay all our ships and cost our owners even more money than the present delay." Silence fell on the meeting as he spoke. "I propose that the Ceylon Government sign an indemnity to meet all losses of the companies concerned." A murmur of agreement rippled round the room. "I can reveal that I had naval experience here during the war as a Lieutenant Commander in HMS *Teviotbank* and I am willing to allow my ship to lead the convoy to the north."

This was acceptable to Commodore Royce de Mal, and all the masters then agreed to take part in the operation provided the indemnity was signed.

Back on the ship John organised the crew to work all night in preparation to receive the passengers. Three 'tween-deck spaces were cleared as well as tarpaulins being spread over the derricks to give shelter. Public rooms were utilised as stores for food and spaces for any sick refugees. Extra water and stores were loaded

91

under the watchful eye of armed soldiers patrolling the docks.

As proposed by John, *Crestbank* was to be the first ship to head northwards and land her passengers. She was supposed to have a naval escort but it never did appear. Altogether 1,067 passengers boarded the ship and this was the largest number carried in any ship from Colombo. These people were brought onto the quay in groups of about 500 and then slowly moved, with their possessions, to their respective ships. While this happened, various British women from the Red Cross and other welfare workers made tea and helped the very frightened refugees in any way they could. During this operation His Excellency the Governor General Sir Oliver Goonetilleke visited the ship to wish the crew well and to watch the food consisting of rice, lentils, pineapples, tinned fruit and fresh bread being loaded.

Just before daylight on the 3rd of June *Crestbank* sailed from the port bound for Kankesanturai. At this time the south-west monsoon made the trip uncomfortable for the early part of the voyage but on board the crew worked hard to make their unfortunate passengers as comfortable as possible. It was to their credit that all on board *Crestbank* arrived without any further incident. At Point Pedro John navigated the Pedro Channel and had disembarked his passengers by the time the other vessels had arrived. Then it was just a matter of sailing back to Colombo and completing his loading for South America.

For his action in this episode John was awarded the MBE in the New Year's Honours' List of 1959. He was a patriotic Cornishman and was very proud to be so honoured by his country. It also proved the final answer to the schoolmaster in St. Ives who, in 1919, said he would never get anywhere. It was to be 1963 before he was able to attend a Royal Investiture with his wife and daughter-in-law, to collect the insignia at Buckingham Palace.

One incident on the 17th of January 1959 did take the gloss off John's voyage in the *Crestbank*. While loading in the port of Necochea, Argentina, homeward bound for the United Kingdom, the second engineer decided to go swimming in the vicinity of the wreck of the SS *Chaco*. Warnings had been issued to the crew not to bathe in this area but Mr Bates went anyway.

Unfortunately the gentleman drowned and his body was never recovered from beneath the wreck. This tragedy left its mark, as John prided himself that his crews normally carried out his orders and respected his judgment, and the paper work and regrets clouded the voyage home to Avonmouth. After an eventful twenty-two months' voyage John returned home to St. Ives and a well-earned leave.

12

A Ferry Boat Man

By 1959 Eric had obtained his second mate's ticket and was serving as third officer in Ellerman Lines. This was one of the few leaves when both John and Eric were home at the same time and there was a lot of good-natured banter about their respective companies and individual careers. Unlike his father, Eric had no intention of serving such long voyages at sea. In fact, he had just returned from a trip to the Persian Gulf and India which had taken eight months. That proved too long a time away from home for him and he was talking of looking for a company which offered shorter voyages. His father was appalled: "You're just a ferry boat man," he would say in disgust. "Whatever is the world coming to?"

One other incident occurred during this leave, which did show the gulf which long voyages created between father and son. One morning, as Eric considered rising from his comfortable bed, his father arrived in the bedroom. He had been up and about for at least an hour and a half and was now keen on organising Eric's life. "Up you get my son," he said. "After breakfast I am going to teach you how to do a jury head knot and you are also going to study your navigation and seamanship for your mate's ticket."

"Oh no I'm not," Eric replied. "I am on leave and you're not the captain in this house, she's in the kitchen."

Eric's mother was soon needed to break up the argument – in

his favour, naturally.

In July John was off on his travels once more as the master of the MV *Eastbank,* with Ann along for the voyage. This vessel had been built in 1947 at Wm Doxford and Sons Limited in Sunderland. She was designed just after the end of the war to run a regular service around the world from the UK to the Gulf of Mexico, then to Australia and New Zealand, before returning home with cargoes of copra from the Pacific Islands.

This 5,947 gross ton vessel had a five cylinder Doxford engine and maintained a service speed of 14 knots. Loading in the Gulf of Mexico, she proceeded to Australia with general cargo. Then followed a number of cargoes of phosphate in Nauru for New Zealand before loading for Rotterdam in the Pacific Islands. The ports of call were in Fiji, Tonga, Tarawa, Samoa, plus the Line Island ports of Fanning, Christmas and Washington. This voyage took just a year and Ann and John arrived in Rotterdam to a surprise.

Eric had asked St. Ives schoolteacher Jill England to marry him and been accepted. He had joined the Palm Line Ltd., for the short voyages of about twelve weeks to West Africa. He was travelling to his first ship in the company at Amsterdam, the MV *Ilorin Palm,* 5,658 gross tons, as second mate, when the *Eastbank* arrived in Rotterdam.

Eric was able to get a day's leave and travel to see his parents and explain his plans for the wedding in August of that year. This, however, was to cause a problem as his father was due to join the *Streambank* in early August. For once his long-suffering wife put her foot down with a vengeance.

"I don't care what the marine superintendent thinks or feels," she retorted to John's protests, "you are staying home for your only son's wedding."

It took about a week of real defiance from Ann before John eventually telephoned the company with his request. It was granted, and while the rest of the crew travelled to the States on the HMS *Queen Elizabeth,* John stayed at home for those few extra days.

It was a memorable event, with father and son both wearing

their Merchant Navy uniforms at the Bedford Road Methodist Chapel in St. Ives. On the day following the wedding, John was flying to the USA while his new daughter-in-law and Eric were flying to Southern Ireland on their honeymoon.

The *Streambank* was still on her maiden voyage at the time, having been completed in November 1958 at Doxford's yard in Sunderland. This fine vessel was to spend another sixteen months under John's command before returning to the UK. She was the largest vessel that John ever commanded. Her gross tonnage was 8,520 tons and her 4-cylinder Doxford engine gave her a speed of 15 knots.

During the voyage she loaded a cargo of Indian products for West Africa and it was there he was to meet Eric in Nigeria at Port Harcourt. Eric was the second mate of a very old steamer called the *Ashanti Palm,* 5,123 gross tons. It was at this meeting that they celebrated the birth of Eric's first son and John's first grandson Ian, on the one night that they were together.

The next day the master of the *Ashanti Palm* and his wife, Captain and Mrs Kopec, and Eric dined on the new Bank Line vessel as John's guests. It was a quite remarkable fact that John was the only married European aboard the *Streambank* at that time and the rest of the officers were celebrating their sailing orders very happily. The ship had just been chartered by Elder Dempster Lines to load a cargo for Philadelphia and New York, before proceeding to the Gulf of Mexico to load for New Zealand, and they had no regrets at not going home, only pleasure in meeting the girls and friends they already had in those countries.

At dinner Captain Kopec complimented John on the efficient service of his stewards and fine condition of the ship. "They don't have Mariners coming on in Britain like this man anymore, he is one of the last of his kind," he told Eric as they returned to their elderly steamer afterwards.

Following this meeting the *Streambank* lifted a huge cargo of groundnuts out of Lagos and then became the first Bank Line vessel to load bags of cocoa at the new port of Tema in Ghana. On sailing from this port John submitted a comprehensive report on all aspects of the visit. It gives very thorough sailing directions, with a safe anchorage position, pilot availability and berthing conditions as well as comments on the dock labour, cranes, stores, fuel and freshwater. All the paper work needed by the port authorities such as immigration, customs, port health and police. Indeed after its circulation through the fleet any Bank Line master would know exactly what to expect at this port.

This voyage was completed at the end of 1961 in Southampton, and following a short coastal trip to London John supervised the pay-off of the crew at the Dock Street shipping office. It is interesting to read his immaculate hand-written accounts for the voyage.

Covering a period of sixteen months and four-days, the total wages accounted for were £16,826.7s.10p, while deductions totalled £14,835.15s.2p. To pay off the British officers he requested £1,849.11s.8p while £141.1s.0p could be retained as wages of deserters. This money was then handed to him at the Bank Line office in Bury Street, London, in a brief-case. He then proceeded back to the ship in a rush hour train full to capacity with home-going Londoners.

"Goodness knows what would have happened if I was robbed or waylaid," he later commented.

In fact he kept copies of all his accounts from every ship that he commanded and took great pride in their accuracy. One story related by Ann clearly shows this from his voyage on the *Eastbank* in July 1960.

On this voyage John calculated his accounts for the company (called the portage bill) as the vessel crossed the Bay of Biscay in really fine weather. Much to his horror the mammoth set of accounts refused to balance by the sum of one penny. Three nights of checking and rechecking the figures did not reveal the tiny mistake, and John was quite deaf to his wife's pleading. "Why don't you put a penny in yourself and come to your bunk," she urged him.

After paying-off in Rotterdam, John and Ann returned to London and all through their stay in a splendid hotel he continued to search for the mistake to no avail. And so a rather grumpy ship's master presented himself at the company's office in Bury

Street with the accounts. A company accountant took the offending set of figures and quietly checked through them for about five minutes.

"Tell me Captain," he said, "did anyone die after you took over a year ago?"

"No," said John, "but an engineer did die two weeks before I joined."

"Yes, I see," said the man. "There was a change in the death benefit and the previous master has worked it twice, with a penny difference."

"Oh good," said John. "My accounts balance then?"

"No Captain. You signed for the ship when you took over and the mistake is logged against you."

It seemed that John was almost impossible to live with for the next week after that incident.

Following the command of the *Streambank* he was next appointed to the MV *Inverbank,* then being built in Doxford's yard at Sunderland. This 6,313 gross ton vessel was to give him a familiar problem while trading in Australian waters. On approaching the pilot station at the entrance to the Torres Strait John had slowed down and stopped the vessel. Unfortunately the starting valve now jammed on the engine and it was unable to move ahead or astern, and with a strong flood tide under the ship she was now rapidly approaching shoal water and could have gone aground. Following a sharp command from John the mate ran to the fo'c'sle and let go both anchors, and the ship pulled up very close to shallow water. The pilot then came aboard demanding to know why the ship had dropped her anchors.

"Thought you would be late pilot, and I just wanted to check all was well with the anchors, this being a new ship," replied John with a very straight face.

All the while the engineers were struggling to get the engine going. If the pilot had realised the true reason for being at anchor, a tug would have been needed as an escort through the narrow channels. Chatting away, John then asked the pilot into the chart-room to look at the chart and tell him all the relevant facts about their passage. While they were there the message was received from the engine room that the ship could now continue. So when the captain and pilot returned to the bridge the anchors were being lifted and all was well.

One interesting incident occurred on this voyage concerning the Indian crew of the ship. According to the official log of the vessel, on the 30th November 1962 the crew refused to accept a supply of cooking oil called 'gee' as it did not smell or look like the oil supplied in Calcutta. It has to be remembered that there was a very different attitude to the crew in those days and John was, if anything, rather old fashioned in his outlook.

At once he mustered all forty-two of the crew on the boat deck and the ship chandler addressed them, explaining that he had supplied 'gee' for many years and it was made from butter and peanut oil and was perfectly normal. After some discussion the crew still refused to use the oil or work until they had an acceptable alternative. This entailed the ship getting butter at an extra cost and the crew refusing to work until it arrived. John was not pleased at this outcome and on his orders a sample of the offending oil was sent for analysis. In the meantime the crew were officially warned that they would be charged the extra cost involved should the 'gee' be found to be normal. It would seem that the result was confirmed in the chandler's favour and the crew were all debited the cost of the butter in their next port, New Orleans. Following a voyage of nineteen months and seventeen days the ship completed her maiden voyage at Avonmouth on the 11th November 1963.

By February 1964 John had returned from leave to stand by a really beautiful new ship, the MV *Weybank*. This 6,378 gross ton motor vessel had five hatches and was built at Harland & Wolff in Belfast. All accommodation was of the highest standard and air-conditioned. It was a very great contrast with the Hain Line vessels John had sailed in at the beginning of his sea career. Now the running of the vessel was almost silent and the navigation equipment had changed fundamentally; and all the crew had a much better life on board with a bar and portable swimming pool.

The ship loaded her first cargo in London, bound for New Guinea. This included 4,000 tons of cement at Bevans Wharf and a 58-ton landing craft, which was lifted on board by the ship's own heavy lift derrick in the old West India dock basin. This craft called the *Vonu* was delivered to Honiara. Finally the ship discharged the cement at Darwin in Australia before proceeding to India with grain, and then loading for South America before returning to the Gulf of New Orleans.

At New Orleans John was joined by his wife Ann and they enjoyed the rest of the voyage bidding their friends good-bye as they looked forward to semi-retirement. After seventeen months, the *Weybank* berthed at Hull and, at the age of sixty, John decided to finish his long voyages and just relieve on the company vessels around the United Kingdom and the Continent.

On a couple of occasions in the next five years John did take ships as far as America, but in the main his days of tramping the world shipping lanes were over. During those five years he was to serve on thirteen Bank Line vessels discharging, dry-docking and loading around the Continent and British ports.

Just one story of this period will suffice to give a flavour of a relieving master's lot in those days.

On 17th July 1969 John was the relieving master on the *Lindenbank,* 6,351 gross tons, at Rotterdam. Orders had been received that the Indian crew were to transfer to another company vessel, *Gowanbank.* Due to reasons beyond the agent's control no suitable craft was ready to transfer the thirty-eight crew members and their gear to the other vessel out in the river at the allotted time of 10am.

The crew was then asked to go by passenger launch, with their effects to follow as soon as a vessel could be found. Needless to say the crew declined and opted to stay with their gear. By 1pm a tug arrived and commenced loading the crew's gear. It was quickly realised that the tug could only take half the crew and a second tug was then ordered. At 2.20pm the first tug left and the second tug began loading. Just about a half hour later this tug was going to leave with all the rest of the crew, when an urgent message arrived from the agents. The transfer of crew had been cancelled and the old crew was required to return to the *Lindenbank*!

100

At once confusion reigned, with the crew on the second tug refusing to move. The first tug then returned and came alongside accompanied by two customs launches. The customs officers explained to John that they were not satisfied with the paper work provided by the agents.

"Oh that's OK," said John to the customs officer. "The transfer has been cancelled and the crew must return to the *Lindenbank*."

"Oh no, sir," explained the customs officer, "while we've got them with all their gear we will search it."

"Right then, carry on and search," said an irritated John.

"We have a problem sir," the customs officer explained, "your crew are not willing to let us search the baggage and will not co-operate. They are also complaining about the lack of consideration and demanding apologies from the captain, agents and customs. Now they are demanding a representative of the Indian Consulate to attend and we have a diplomatic incident."

John laughed. " It will be impossible to get an Indian diplomat at this time," he said. "Any dispute with them over searching is your problem. I will make any explanations to the crew tomorrow when I sort this out."

"In that case, Captain, we shall detain your crew on the tugs until they co-operate."

"You must do what you must do," said John. "Would you like a beer?"

"No thank you," said the officer, "we will stay with the crew on the tug and customs vessels."

With all sides refusing to listen, John retired to his cabin, opened a beer, and waited.

It was over four hours later that the customs weakened and agreed to let the crew come back aboard the ship, but the crew was still determined to keep their protest going. John eventually persuaded them to board the *Lindenbank* with a promise that senior members of the crew could visit the Indian consul's office next day to air their grievances. This was finally agreed as the clock ticked on to midnight and order was restored.

For most of the voyages during this period Ann accompanied my John and they really enjoyed this time together. On one memorable occasion John was in command of the *Sprucebank*, some 6,163 gross tons, in May 1969. As his ship approached Land's End, Eric was serving on the Trinity House vessel *Stella*, 1,546 gross tons, and had his son Ian on board as they sailed from Penzance to change the crew on the *Seven Stones Light Vessel*. They passed each other off the Longships lighthouse just before midnight. Ian and Eric were able to talk to John and Ann on the radio and Eric exchanged a message with the ship by aldis lamp in short and long flashes in the Morse code. When he arrived home John wanted to know who had sent the message by lamp. "I did," Eric said, "no one else uses that form of communication any longer."

"That's funny," John said, "I was the only one on my ship able to do it. The Merchant Navy has gone to pot son."

Finally, in December 1970, John, in his own words: "Swallowed the anchor after fifty years at sea and came ashore for the last time."

Both John and Ann enjoyed a long retirement of twenty-five years. They regularly travelled around the country to see old seafarer friends and enjoy the sights of Great Britain. John became a Trinity House Sub Commissioner of Pilotage for the ports of Hayle and St. Ives. His examination of new pilots was vigorous and demanding, as Eric his son was to find out when he applied for a licence for this pilotage district.

At one stage he had the privilege, as he put it, to serve as relieving mate of the Scillonian ferry *Queen Of the Isles*, which Eric commanded at the time. This was to allow the serving chief officer to have a medical examination.

His talks to local societies about his times at sea were well attended and appreciated, and his lively interest in the local St. Ives Museum focused mainly on the well-stocked Hain Room. It gave him much pleasure in the last year of his life to show the wife of his old *Trevessa* companion Douglas Bell round the museum. Lady Bell was charmed at his old world courtesy and long memory. He also still carried out the odd duty for the Bank Line, representing the company at a *Foylebank* Association reunion at Portland in April 1978.

In the later years of their retirement John devotedly looked after Ann who was failing in health. In 1991 they celebrated their sixtieth wedding anniversary with a big party in a local restaurant. He was to celebrate the birth of his great-grandson Sam, Eric's youngest son Jeremy's boy, in 1993. But in 1995 Ann's death really devastated him and he passed away on the ninth of January 1999, exactly seventy-eight years from the day he went to sea.

*   *   *   *

Author's Endpiece:

In writing this book as a tribute to my father I discovered the following maxim lodged in his wallet. It is a good example of his sense of humour and I must admit brought a smile to my face as I read it:

A Captain is a man who knows a great deal about very little. He goes on knowing more and more about less and less until he finally knows practically everything about nothing.

A Chief Engineer, on the other hand, is a man who knows very little about a great deal. He keeps on knowing less and less about more and more until he knows nothing about everything.

A Ship's Agent starts out knowing practically everything about everything. He winds up knowing practically nothing about everything due to his association with Captains and Chief Engineers.